Praise for *Why We Read*

"Delightful reminiscences of a book lover."

—Kirkus Reviews

"Shannon Reed gives us grace to love the books we love and reminds us, by sharing her own tender memories, why certain stories stick in our hearts for a lifetime. Shannon is one of my favorite writers—brilliant, humble, and wickedly funny. I envy her students and will return to these pages again and again. And I'm thrilled that she officially let me off the hook for never reading *Middlemarch*."

—Elizabeth Passarella, author of
Good Apple* and *It Was an Ugly Couch Anyway

"*Why We Read* is a rare thing—a joy on its own, as well as potent inspiration to revisit the formative books from your own reading journey. Shannon Reed's warm, authentic voice in these invigorating essays invites us into her literary universe while at the same time encouraging us to expand our own. I cannot wait to gift this marvelous book to all the readers in my life."

—Caitlin Kunkel, coauthor of
New Erotica for Feminists: Satirical Fantasies of Love, Lust, & Equal Pay

"What a charming book Shannon Reed has written, a love letter (or series of love letters) to reading as avocation and as art. The title, of course, is both question and declaration, and in response, Reed offers a variety of takes on why we read. In the end, there is no answer, which is only as it should be; reading is too capacious to be pinned down. Better, as Reed illustrates throughout here, to consider it a process, undertaken on no terms other than its own."

—David L. Ulin, author of *The Lost Art of Reading*

"The more I know about Shannon Reed, the more I like her. This is a rich, funny, poignant book, and the author will be your new best friend."

—Mary Norris, *New York Times* bestselling author of
Between You and Me: Confessions of a Comma Queen

"Shannon Reed's *Why We Read* offers an entertaining, life-affirming, and laugh-out-loud funny response to 'how do I love thee, let me count the ways' for those of us who always have a book within arm's reach. And for anyone in your life who has until now resisted the restorative charm of reading, *Why We Read* is the perfect gift."

—**Annabelle Gurwitch**, *New York Times* **bestselling author of** *You're Leaving When? Adventures in Downward Mobility*

"*Why We Read* is deeply delightful—a hug of a book that will remind you that there is simply nothing better than the King's Pastime. OK, I made that up, no one calls reading the King's Pastime—but they should, because it's the most sublime way to spend your time, and Shannon's funny, heart-tugging prose reminded me precisely why."

—**Jen Spyra, author of** *Big Time: Stories*

WHY WE READ

ON BOOKWORMS, LIBRARIES
and Just One More Page
BEFORE LIGHTS OUT

SHANNON REED

HANOVER
SQUARE
PRESS

**HANOVER
SQUARE
PRESS™**

Recycling programs
for this product may
not exist in your area.

ISBN-13: 978-1-335-00796-4

Why We Read

Copyright © 2024 by Shannon Reed

Some names and identifying characteristics have been changed.

An earlier version of "How I Choose a Book: A Thirteen-Step Guide" was published in *Oh Reader*.

"Signs You May Be a Female Character in a Work of Historical Fiction" was originally published at McSweeney's Internet Tendency.

"Questions I Use to Evaluate a New Recipe" was originally published at NewYorker.com.

An earlier version of "To Make Us Cry (II)" was originally published in the *Paris Review*.

Grateful acknowledgments are made to Sheri Holman for permission to use an excerpt from her novel *The Dress Lodger* and Richard Katrovas for permission to excerpt his poem "Kings' Day, 1984."

TM and ® are trademarks of Harlequin Enterprises ULC.

Hanover Square Press
22 Adelaide St. West, 41st Floor
Toronto, Ontario M5H 4E3, Canada
HanoverSqPress.com
BookClubbish.com

Printed in U.S.A.

For Mum-mum, who taught me to read, the best gift ever,
And for Dad, who loved books,
And for Mom, who still takes me to the library,
And for Justin, who read alongside me on so many trips,
And for my students, with whom I most love talking about books.

Also, always, thank you, Roo.

Also by Shannon Reed

Why Did I Get a B? And Other Mysteries We're Discussing in the Faculty Lounge

WHY WE READ

Love's a thing that's gathered, chance by chance

—"Love and the Years," Alfred Allen

TABLE OF CONTENTS

Preface: Why I Read   11

To Get to Go to the Library   19

How I Choose a Book: A Thirteen-Step Guide   33

Because There Was Always Another Page   37

To Finish a Series   41

Calmed-Down Classics of American Literature
for the Anxiety-Ridden   49

Because We Had To   51

To Break the Rules   63

Signs You May Be a Female Character in a
Work of Historical Fiction   71

To Learn About (and From) the Past   75

For Love   85

Signs You May Be a Character in a
Popular Children's Book   93

To Make Us Cry   97

Because I Wanted Free Pizza   103

To Find the Main Point   111

Because Failure Is Most Definitely an Option   123

But Not Shakespeare!   133

Signs You May Be a Character in a
Shakespearean Play   141

To Feel Less Alone   143

To See Ourselves Across Time   151

Signs You May Be an Adult Character in
a YA Novel   161

To Taste   165

Questions I Use to Evaluate a New Recipe   175

Because Someone Gave Me a Book   179

For Comfort   185

To Feel Superior   193

To Be Shocked   207

Town Summer Festival Kickoff
Declared "Success"   219

To Learn There's More Than a Single Story   223

Because It's Fun   229

To Save My Life   243

To Shake Up Your Perspective   255

The Five People You Meet When You
Work in a Bookstore   263

Because Someone Is Paying You to Teach a
Class about Vampires   265

To Learn How to Die (and How to Live)   281

Because Once More Was Enough   289

To Try Again   293

To Motivate Us   301

To Make Us Cry (II)   305

Because We Are What We Read   309

List of Books and Works Mentioned   313

Acknowledgments   325

WHY I READ

I don't remember a time when I didn't know how to read. My grandmother, an elementary-school teacher, taught me when I was two. "You were ready" was Mum-mum's matter-of-fact response the one time I asked her why. Two is before my memories really begin, young enough to make reading seem less a hobby and more a way of life. I breathed, I ate, I cried, I slept, I chattered, I read. And I have not stopped reading since.

When I ask my creative writing students at the University of Pittsburgh to tell me stories about themselves as readers, I hear anecdotes like that one. They, too, were constantly exhorted by nearby adults to put their books down and look around on family trips (I nearly missed spotting Old Faithful in Yellowstone because I was nose-deep in a *Nancy Drew*). They, too, chose reading over most other activities, and, like me, many were punished for minor infractions by having books taken away for a day, leaving us to watch television—

the horror!—for entertainment. They, too, packed and still pack multiple books for any trips of more than a city block in distance (although e-readers have saved all of our backs, thankfully). Like me, they read and continue to read at any and all lulling moments of life: on the toilet, brushing one's teeth, in line at the post office, on any form of public transportation, by audiobook when driving.

Like the Russian proverb about how one fisherman spots another from one hundred yards away, I feel a familial affection for my fellow longtime, intense readers. We are kin. Quiet, introspective, tea-and-cozy-quilt-loving kin.

While some of my students are finding their way back to reading for pleasure, I never stopped. I still read while I brush my teeth, squinting my middle-aged eyes inches from the book, and still bring three times the number of books I could possibly read on any trip, including my daily commute to campus. I still visit the library—okay, two different libraries—every week. It's truly one of the greatest honors that the librarians recognize me on sight and start checking out my books on hold when I walk in. All these years later, I still define myself as a reader.

In writing this book, I've come to realize perhaps the most important reason I've remained so: the act of reading makes me feel safe. Not the book itself—paperback, hardcover, e-, I truly do not care—but the exercise of running my eyes over the words. The translation from symbol into meaning. The direct, pleasant diction of the voice inside my head. The influx of information. The transport to other lives, other worlds.

I've had other identities all my life: Gloria and Ron's daughter, Justin's sister, Kathryn and Henry and Violet's granddaughter, Andrew's best friend, Linda and Pete and Nedra and Gladys's niece, a teacher, a teammate, a colleague, a confidante, a godmama, a PK (pastor's kid), a cis-gender girl, a reader, a writer, a knitter, a baker, a *Muppets Take Manhattan* superfan, and also a hearing-impaired person. For unknown genetic reasons, my father's mother (Violet) was profoundly hard of hearing, my father was slightly better off, and I am slightly better off than him. I don't have children. The genetic quirk ends with me.

Some of my childhood was stressful because I was hearing-impaired. I grew up in the 1980s and '90s, in a world where authority figures expected to have their orders—their *verbally* given orders—followed. I can recall incidents large and small when I was unable to clearly hear some adult and was punished for it. In preschool, I was kept back from recess because I wasn't closing my eyes during prayers (I was reading the teacher's lips, a skill that none of the involved people, including me, understood to exist). In middle school, an English teacher made me repeat a tongue twister while standing in front of the class for five agonizing minutes, unaware that I wasn't pronouncing the *S*s I couldn't hear. In music class, I couldn't identify a piece from the first few notes unless I was seated practically on top of the record player, ruining my grades on listening quizzes. In French class, I truly had no idea how to say anything at all beyond *Bonjour* (which I probably said incorrectly).

I liked people, but outside my family and close friends, I found them stress-inducing. Some were soft-spoken, many were offended when asked to repeat themselves, and all occasionally told me to "just forget it" rather than say something again. I often missed what was said on television and in

films in the days before closed captioning, regularly nodded
in agreement when someone whispered something to me, no
matter what it might have been, and more than once gave a
stranger incorrect directions rather than admit I wasn't quite
sure what they wanted.

But *reading*! That I could do. When I read, I felt smart.
And in reading, I was never lonely, the way I sometimes felt
in real life. Reading did not lead me astray. The words were
clear, and if I didn't understand them, it wasn't because I didn't
hear them correctly. No one cared if I reread (asked the book
to repeat, that is) multiple times. And people mostly left me
alone when my nose was buried in a book. Reading was always safe and always good company.

Over the years, I've developed a strong inclination toward
reading as my preferred way to learn new information. My
father was just the opposite, always an audio learner, pre-
ferring to ask strangers rather than read anything. Once, in
London, I watched him lean over a barrier on the bus (past
the *Do Not Lean Over Barrier* sign) to ask the driver a question (despite the *Do Not Talk to the Driver* sign) and sighed
with exasperation when he could not then hear the answer.[1]
In the time it took him to do that, I had read not just those
two signs but another that provided the information he was
seeking. I couldn't understand why he didn't rely on reading.

Of course, the driver turned out to be delighted to chat with
him, and we ended up visiting an excellent restaurant that man
recommended, so clearly reading only gets you so far. As I've

---

1   He expected me to hear it, instead, which was its own set of problems. Bless
    our hearts, for some reason the hearing-impaired never expect anyone else
    to be, too.

gotten older, I've learned that verbal information-gathering[2] isn't always so bad. But still, reading was and is my preference. I detest being read aloud to. I scramble to get a printed copy of the PowerPoint when a few are made available. I'd prefer to turn off the sound all together before I'd give up my closed captions on TV. I love the chat box on Zoom. When I read, I feel about 95 percent sure I'm getting the nuance, meaning, and portent of what's being conveyed. When required to listen, I perceive maybe 85 percent, but probably more like 70 percent in a group setting without amplification.

Over my lifetime, things have changed, slowly, very slowly, but surely. For someone of my persuasion, who detested phone calls not merely with a Gen Xer's ambivalence but because they were inadequate conveyors of information I needed— more than once, I simply hung up when I couldn't hear the person on the other end, brave little toaster that I am—the rise of online forms and contacts and information has been delicious. I feel very sure that I would not have a writing career if I hadn't been able to communicate by email and shared documents. The idea of being a writer as it used to be done, by drinking whiskey sours with editors at the Carlyle or whatever, gives me the willies. Thankfully, for all that we bemoan the way people consume fewer books now, we collectively read much more, I think, and communicate that way, too. My students tell me "I don't read anymore" with utter sincerity, and then turn back to their phones and laptops to read away. We all read, all the time. Just perhaps not books.

But I have never lost my affection for and my dependency

---

2   This makes me sound like a robot. I mean *chatting*.

on them. This is where I pull away from the pack of fellow bookworms, I sense. Much as I like videos and reels and whatever new thing has been invented by the time this goes to print, I'm always reaching back to the OG form, the book, looking for what I can read to help me understand. Reading a book is quiet, clear, and organized. It's not hard. It waits until I am ready, pauses when I need a break, and is still happy to repeat. Reading absolutely never says "Just forget it" when I need clarification. It doesn't care how I pronounce the words in my head (or aloud, for that matter). It never makes me feel worse and rarely makes me feel lonely. Reading gives me the world.

And that, friends, is why *I* read.

But here, I want to dig into a bigger question, the one implicit in the title: Why do *we* read? Why do *you*? I've bitten through to the chewy nougat core of my personal answer above. In the rest of the book, I invite you to consider myriad other ways to answer the question. Sometimes we read for comfort. Sometimes to feel superior. Sometimes to learn. Sometimes because we are told to. Sometimes out of love, sometimes out of jealousy, sometimes to feel better. There are many answers, only a few of which I can unpack here, but it's been fun to try.

I've been unofficially researching those answers for quite some time. For over twenty years, I've been teaching others how to read, in various ways. First, in preschool classrooms in Pennsylvania and Manhattan; then, at Stella Maris, a little Catholic high school for girls on the beach in Queens, which I am sorry to say is no longer around; then at a public high school in Brooklyn (which I call THSB in this book, for the Theater High School of Brooklyn, a pretty close approximation of its name); and, now, finally, as a teaching associate professor in the creative writing program, part of the English department at Pitt. In that time, I've worked with thousands (yikes!) of students, from the most enthusiastic readers—young adults with bookish tattoos—to those who would have opted to eat dirt rather than read *A Wrinkle in Time* if they could've. I do not have grand lessons in how to convert the latter to the former, but I have learned a great deal about why we read (and why we don't) from them, which I share here.

In fact, I've structured the book in a very rough chronological order, moving you from my own childhood reading to my education and through my teaching career. I've also plopped in a bit of reading-adjacent humor because what I love, I (gently) mock. I wouldn't say I make jokes at books' expense, exactly, but I do start to run a tab. Whenever possible, I try to urge you, dear reader, back to and further into reading, dismissing every single reason why you don't read more. At least I hope I make a good try at that. Reading has brought me so much pleasure, every day of my life since Mum-mum got me started, that I can't help but want you to feel that joy, too.

I hope this serves as a celebration of books and reading... and libraries and poetry and looking forward to cross-country trips (pretty much just because you get to read in the backseat) and visiting used bookstores and Amish romances and the pets of Hollywood's stars and vampire lesbians from the 1800s, too. Reading has been my closest companion. Writing this has felt like a chance to celebrate (and roast) our 45+-year anniversary. I'm so happy to champion its endless charms here with you.

TO GET TO GO TO
THE LIBRARY

I am five or six. I've been going to the public library in Mechanicsburg, Pennsylvania, with my parents since before I can remember. I love it there, and long with all of my stubborn little heart to be allowed to take out more than two or three books at a time, since I must share my mom's account and there is a book limit. One day, my mom takes me to the checkout counter where the smiling librarian asks me a series of simple questions and then gives me a card to sign. That one gets filed, and another is handed to me, my name neatly printed on it. My first library card. It is a *junior* library card, I am informed, to be used only in the *children's* section. No John Irving novels for me! It's the first form of identification I have ever owned, and I am flush with pride at this proof of my existence and independence. I have my own book limit now! I put the card in my otherwise completely empty Snoopy wallet, treasuring the expanse of books, and life, ahead of me.

I am eight or nine. I'm in front of the shelves in the children's section in the same library, trying to decide between two books. I always choose carefully, due to that limit, for the books have to sustain me for seven full days, until we return. I favor thick books, which make for longer reading. I am against pictures in books, which do not.

A boy, probably twelve years old, appears next to me, too close. I shrink away from him, uneasy. Suddenly, he wordlessly grabs my tote bag.

I cling to the straps, as I lurch forward, scrambling to keep the bag on my shoulder. I throw the books I had been considering behind me, to protect them.

"Hey! That's my bag!" I whisper urgently at him. (You shouldn't yell in the library, even when under attack.) He gives it another tug, pulling it off my shoulder, the bag now between us, each of us holding on for dear life. Using whatever muscle tone I had developed through my exercise regimen of reading all day except when choreographing dances to *Flashbeagle* in the basement, I yank it back, which knocks him off balance, but he keeps holding on. I'm using my mom's plasticized cotton tote bag from England, decorated with a charming charcoal sketch of sheep. As I grip, I wonder why this kid so badly wants that bag, of all the bags? But no matter. That bully is not. Going. To. Take. My. Books.

He yanks so hard I start to fall forward, but I dig in my heels and yell, "Stop it, you mean boy!" which finally wins the attention of the librarian across the room with her back to us. As she hustles over to intervene, the boy gives up and runs, half slamming into the glass door and starting to cry

on his way out of the children's room. I have won! The de-
fender of my castle!

To celebrate, I check out both books. I deserve them.

I am fourteen years old. We have moved to a suburb of
Johnstown, Pennsylvania, and all four of us—me, Mom, Dad,
and my younger brother, Justin—love to visit the local library,
this one a tiny nook on the first floor of a small strip mall/
apartment complex, within walking distance of our home if
we are particularly motivated. After establishing my book-nerd
credentials by winning the library's Halloween mask-making
contest (I decorated my mask with quilling,[3] my other principal
hobby, which I taught myself from a book. Have I mentioned
that I was a weird kid?), I'm invited to join the elite teenage
page program, which will pay me a whopping three dollars an
hour. I will work about five hours a week.

Fifteen dollars more a week is not nothing when you're
fourteen in 1988, but mostly, I just love the intimacy with
the library the job gives me. At first, I shelve books, repair
books, and, occasionally, with much sadness discard books,
which really means bringing some of them home to live out
their days piled under an R.E.M. poster in my bedroom.
As I prove myself to have decent interpersonal skills, I'm allowed to check out and renew books for patrons, help them
find the books they want on the shelves (which occasionally
means assisting a classmate, improving my social standing),
and teach them how to use our reference sources, such as the
Index of Periodical Literature, a compendium of green leather-

---

3   Of course you know this, but quilling is the ancient art of rolling thin strips
     of paper into delicate filigree.

bound volumes that list every article in every major magazine by year, which is quite possibly my favorite thing in the entire place. During my downtime, generally the half hour before the library closes, I look up R.E.M. and U2 in the periodical index and pull the magazines with articles on them to read. At other times, I listen to the patrons' compliments and complaints; in the days before a reserve system, there's a lot of grousing that the latest Scott Turow or John Grisham is never in. As I grow into the job, I start recommending books. Every once in a while, a patron will tell me that they loved the book I'd suggested, and I feel a particular pleasure: I've introduced a friend to a friend. On those days, I sometimes walk down the hill to our house in the twilight feeling like I'm simply traveling from one home to another.

I am seventeen, with only a few months left until I graduate. The little library has moved into a brand-new, larger building, closer to the high school I attend, and I'm now getting paid five dollars an hour as a page there. It's a lovely, airy space, although it has a strange smell that I assume will fade with time. There are many distinct touches to the building, both good and bad. There's a brick mosaic in the entryway, in a style I've never seen anywhere else, which is lovely. But the drop-off window is shoved into a strange corner, which requires backing up into a busy parking lot after dropping books off, so no one uses it, which is less lovely.

Our beloved director retires, and a new woman is hired who, for reasons I still don't know, doesn't like me. It's possible she doesn't like anyone. She does her best to make my work life unpleasant, always harping on me to work faster (I work fast enough, it's not the Ford assembly line) or stop daydreaming in the stacks (that's fair, I did do that). Just as she starts to campaign in earnest for me to be fired, I realize that I truly no longer have time for the job and quit, which she apparently sees as a victory until she realizes that I will be returning to the library—*my* library—to take out and return books on a weekly basis, and now she has to wait on me. She leaves the job soon after for reasons that do not involve me. I still go to the building every few months with my mom, who still lives in Johnstown and stops there weekly. Thirty years later, it smells the same, but now that smell makes me feel like I've come home.

I'm eighteen, at college. There is no end to the beautiful spaces made available to me on Otterbein University's campus. As a theater major, I'm given access to mirror-lined dance studios, rehearsal rooms nearly filled by grand pianos, and classrooms in ivy-covered buildings. It's overwhelming. I don't feel I fit in at any of these places.

During our first week of classes, one assignment or another sends me to the library, and wandering around, completely flummoxed by the unexpected lack of the Dewey decimal system—my polestar, lo these many years—I stumble upon the magazine section. I find out later they are technically *journals*, not merely magazines, but no matter. There are long, broad tables, comfy leather-clad chairs, and there, to my left, stretches the green line of the years-long collection of the *Index of Periodical Literature*. I'm home.

I'm twenty-two. At my first real job, as a news reporter for a talk-radio station in Altoona, Pennsylvania, I'm a lost toy: a liberal in a world of conservatives, the youngest by at least twenty years, and deeply ill-suited for the work of asking upset people how they feel at the scenes of their tragedies. Although I was born there, Altoona feels unwelcoming, too far from my family to see them every day, but too close by to not want to. Again, the public library saves me. Within days of moving to my (retrospectively, supercute) apartment in downtown Altoona, I visit the public library and load up on books. At the checkout, I ask to apply for a library card and present my electric bill as proof that someone has allowed me to rent a place on my own, as if I am an adult.

"Shannon Reed," the librarian says. "From the radio?"

I nod, surprised. My boss had suggested that I choose a radio name, but then said, "but your real name is so good," so I didn't bother.

"I listen to you do the news all the time," the librarian says, and she makes sure I have both a public library tote bag and a free bookmark, clearly delighted that someone as famous as me would deign to visit the public library.

Of course, I go back weekly, until the radio station comes to its senses and lays me off, and I move back to Johnstown. I am not recognized in public again for over twenty years.

I'm twenty-three. Newly hired to teach at the preschool in the basement of my dad's church—nepotism much?—I begin making weekly trips to the Highland Library to pick out books to read to my students. The supervising teachers break the school year down into units, and then weeks within those units, so I know to look for books about apples, or pumpkins, or Halloween, or bread. I very much appreciate this simplified approach to the passage of time. New books have arrived in my years away, of course, but much of the selection is the same as when I was shelving it. I can instinctively locate *Strega Nona* or *The Wheels on the Bus* or *The Snowy Day* on the correct shelf within seconds. I'm proud of this.

I'm twenty-five and have moved to New York City to get my master's in education. I'm put in a graduate student apartment in the West Village—woo!—and wander around on my first full day of living there. Turning the corner from my block on Eleventh Street to Sixth Avenue, I spot a stunning brick building. It's striped, with a soaring clock tower. It's not a church, I can tell, but it feels like a spiritual home of some kind. I'm drawn down the street by its beauty, and gobsmacked to realize that it's the nearest branch of the New York Public Library.

I hurry home to fetch the only piece of mail I have with my new address on it—a card my thoughtful mom sent to have waiting for me—and rush back to the library with it. Although it's obviously not the required mail from ConEd or Verizon or some other official authority, and although the librarian is not visibly charmed by my rushed explanation that I had moved less than twenty-four hours ago but need books to make my new apartment feel like home, I am allowed to get my first NYPL card. He even advises me on where to find the new books and that the bathrooms are in the basement, down the long, spiraling staircase.

Eventually, I'll learn that the majestic building was once the Jefferson Market Courthouse, completed in 1877, made of red brick, yellow sandstone, and white granite. Designed by Frederick Clarke Withers in the high Victorian Gothic style, it was declared one of the five most beautiful buildings in America in 1885. Alas, it fell into disuse and was almost torn down in the 1950s but—huzzah!—the community saved it. It reopened as a library in 1967 and was added to the National Register of Historic Places in 1972. Although it has been targeted for closure several times since, the library has stayed open, continuing to be a beloved fixture of the neighborhood.

Fifteen years later, I will be assigned to read Grace Paley's short story "Wants" in class. It begins, "I saw my ex-husband in the street. I was sitting on the steps of the new library." Although I had (and continue to have) no particular reason to assume that the library Paley uses as her setting is the Jefferson Market Branch, I always picture it so, and thus, this story is one of my very favorites, in the way one loves stories about one's home.

I am thirty-four and have just left Stella Maris, the little beachside Catholic high school for girls in Rockaway, to teach at THSB, a public high school in South Brooklyn. Everything about my first few days is chaos, and I'm not able to look around the enormous building my small school takes up a tiny part of until the first Friday of the semester. On my lunch break, I follow the signs not to the Gymnasia (the plural of *gymnasium*, immediately my new favorite word, and one which I will always take any opportunity to use, including here) but to the Library. When I arrive there, the space makes my heart hurt. Although this isn't possible, the entire room somehow appears to be listing: shelves are empty if not broken, books are ancient if not half-destroyed. Graffiti covers the tables and chairs. The windows, once meant to provide a view across Flatbush Avenue, possibly as far as Jamaica Bay, are frosted-over and barred. There is no one around; the building doesn't have a librarian. I startle a roach.

I can't help but think of the sweet little library at Stella Maris, where Bob was the friendly librarian, where the girls learned how to research, where we faculty stayed late twice a year to read and grade Regents exams while we snacked on pretzels and homemade cookies. I miss it. This place is nothing like that one.

I will bring my students here, occasionally, in the four coming years, but this always seems like a hopeless endeavor, more a daydream than a real belief that this library can be of any help. I stop doing even this when one student folds her arms at the entrance and says, "Is this all they think we deserve? I know what a real library looks like!"

She's right.

I am thirty-six. For the prior ten years, I've lived in a rent-controlled apartment in Park Slope—lucky, lucky, lucky—and every week, I walk to the Central Branch of the Brooklyn Public Library on Flatbush and Eastern Parkway at Grand Army Plaza. Had I been running a Most Beautiful Library Branch in New York contest, the Jefferson Market location would have been very hard to beat, but the Central Branch would have placed. It's worth googling, a stunning building designed to look like a three-story open book, with Art Deco styling. Walking up the low steps to the main entrance—as I almost always did—I enter through fifty-foot bronze doors, bestrewn with gold carvings of American literary characters: Moby Dick, Huck Finn, and Poe's raven, among them.

The sad state of THSB's library continues to eat away at me, knowing, as I do, how much comfort a library can be, how much succor, how much *help* it can provide. I try to encourage my students to go to their local libraries, but only a few are interested. When a colleague and I are given permission to take our seniors on a field trip to the Brooklyn Museum, which is just a short walk west of the Central library branch, I decide to surreptitiously march our thirty teenagers to the library and introduce them to its many charms. I even coax a librarian into explaining how they can get library cards that very day. Only a half dozen of them end up doing so, and I know Calvin only agrees because I say I will give him gum if he does. But still, six new library cards! For the price of one stick of gum! I'm pleased. And apparently, no one bothers reporting my strange, semi-kidnapping to our principal, not even the bus driver, who had to wait an extra forty-five minutes for us, so I got away with it.

A couple of years later, when I am visiting that library after moving away—I try to stop by when I'm in town, make new friends, keep the old, etc.—I think I spot one of those six students studying in the reading room. I'm not sure, and I don't want to interrupt her, but I am heartened all day that perhaps she found a home, too. It cheers me still.

I am thirty-eight years old. I don't like my life and have decided that getting an MFA in creative writing might be the way to build a new one. (I am, eventually, correct.) The only school to accept me into their program is the University of Pittsburgh, and though they have not offered me a full scholarship, and I won't attend without one, I agree to visit the campus in April and meet the faculty. One of the professors takes me and another visiting accepted student, Mitch, to the main branch of the Carnegie Library of Pittsburgh, which is across the street from Pitt's Cathedral of Learning, where the English department is located. Our meeting is unpleasant for me, as the professor seems very intent on getting Mitch to say he'll be taking them up on their offer of a full scholarship. I feel vaguely dismissed.

But the library itself provides some comfort. I love that there is a café within it. I love that the atrium floods with sunlight. It has a room devoted to new releases, and it displays a jigsaw puzzle, collectively worked upon. There are many signs guiding me to categories of authors and genres— African American, LGBTQ+, fantasy, cookbooks, zines— showing an unexpectedly progressive side to Pittsburgh.

After failing to pin Mitch down, our group splits up, and I wander around the building, happening upon a sign noting that August Wilson, the great playwright and son of Pittsburgh, had, in his own words, completed his education at this very library, having dropped out of high school at seventeen. This pleases me. Walking back to check out the fiction shelves, I stop short, seeing out the window a—is that a…?—yes, it's a dinosaur. Its skeleton, anyway. It turns out that from the back rooms of the library, you can peer down into the Carnegie Museum of Natural History's dinosaur exhibit. This place, I think, is magical. I'm sorry it won't be mine.

Many years later, I finally realize that the professor, now my colleague, was trying so hard to get Mitch to say *yes* or *no* because I was their second choice for the full ride. If he had said *no*, she was authorized to immediately offer it to me, which is a scene I like to imagine. After he finally declines several days later, they make me the same offer, and, unlike Mitch, I cannot refuse. Five months later, I take the bus onto campus, meet my new classmates, and, of course, check out a dozen books with my new card. The library already feels like home.

I am forty-six years old. My first book is coming out in the middle of a global pandemic. Nothing feels like it should, and while I and my family and friends are safely locked down, I don't feel much joy at releasing the book into our deeply scary and troubled times. I miss so much: teaching in person, going to church, going to shows, trips to New York, visiting my mom without worry, seeing my friends, and more, but I've found ways to substitute for those, at least for the moment. But nothing replaces going to the library. I miss the Monroeville Public Library, where I've been faithfully picking up my on-hold books for eight years, so very much. When they figure out a way to allow us to take books out again— we order them online, then drive to the library, then wait for the pick-up room to be empty, then, masked and gloved, scurry in, collect our already-checked-out books, and scurry back out—I feel like I might be able to make it through this strange time, after all.

I am forty-seven years old, nearly forty-eight. Halfway through the spring semester, Pitt decides we can hold classes in person, and I meet my students in our classroom for the first time. I've had some of them in two or three courses but have not actually laid eyes on them before. I keep remarking on how everyone is taller than I expected. It's a good day, and when my classes finish, I take the familiar and beloved walk out of the doors of the Cathedral (Cathy, we call her, affectionately) and across Forbes Avenue to the library, passing by the very table where I felt neglected almost precisely ten years ago. It seems so funny to me now.

The new books, as always, are calling me, and I stroll through that section, picking up a cookbook, a memoir, a book about New York, of course. I think about looking for a novel in the fiction section. Turning, just out of the corner of my eye, I spot a familiar pop of yellow: it's my book. Somehow, two years after it came out, it's still getting shelved in the new-books section, which is absurd, except that time did sort of stop for two years, didn't it?

A smarter author would move her book to display it more prominently, or snap a photo to post on Instagram, or grab the nearest librarian in celebration. But I just stare at it, shocked and pleased. Hours later, at my house, I'll realize that what I felt was the surprise of seeing something I made in one of my homes, without my having brought it there.

HOW I CHOOSE A BOOK: A THIRTEEN-STEP GUIDE

1. Determine the genre of the book I would be in the mood to read. (For example, *a gossipy memoir by a minor but well-connected historical figure.*)

2. Head to the bookstore. Greet, by name, the bookseller on duty and pretend I don't see her rubbing her hands together with glee, for today her selling goal will surely be met.

3. Pick up a book that looks very good but is not a gossipy memoir by a minor but well-connected historical figure. Sort of forget about the original book I was hoping to find.

4. Open the new book to a random page and begin to read. Is there anything displeasing (overuse of *-ly* adverbs, the word *impactful*, too many one-sentence paragraphs)? If not, go to #5. If yes, go to #6.

5. Read the book's cover blurbs. Excellent: no blurb is from an author I have some sort of one-sided beef with. Go to #6.

6. Stare at the book cover for a long second and then decide, *eh, might as well take it.* Not quite what I was looking for, but is it likely that at some future point I'll be interested in reading a history of medieval plumbing? Sure, why not? Add it to my stack.

7. Repeat steps 3 through 6 five to eight more times.

8. Finally remember that the point was to find a gossipy memoir by a minor but well-connected historical figure. Look around for the memoir section. Inevitably find myself near the cookbook section, a moth to a flame. Find three cookbooks.

9. When the bookseller offers to take the twelve books I am currently juggling up to the counter, ask her about gossipy memoirs by minor but well-connected historical figures. As she leads me to the correct section, find two more books of interest. No time to stop and vet them, so just toss them to her, too.

10. Now finally in the correct section, find three gossipy/ minor/well-connected memoirs and add them to the stack at the counter which, please God, the bookseller has started to process for me.

11. Pay for all of the books, plus an additional book-themed tote bag, plus a bookmark with a hedgehog on it, plus, if

available, a Jane-Austen-themed soap kept right up by the register. Waddle out to the car, dragging half my body-weight in books. Pretend not to hear bookseller crowing, "Tonight, we're having lobster for dinner!" into her phone.

12. Lovingly unpack/restack and admire all of my new books at home. Shelve them, leaving the memoirs on my table, since I'm *so* ready for some minor historical gossip! Which to choose, which to choose?

13. Realize two hours later that I am reading *Bel Canto* for the seventeenth time.

BECAUSE THERE WAS
ALWAYS ANOTHER PAGE

The hours after you're supposed to be asleep feel crisper, somehow, the weft of the night's loom strung with straw, not yarn. Everything is sharp when there's nothing to pull your attention away: the phone doesn't ring, no one yells for you to please come downstairs for dinner, and the television down the hall is silent since your father's finally finished watching the game. You're the only one still awake. It could feel lonely, but it doesn't because you're not alone. You have an evening companion: your book. You're reading. There's nothing else to do except sleep, which has no appeal, not until you know what happens after Jo cuts off all of her hair.

Outside, summer creeps along in its muggy heaviness, or winter snows crisp and glisten, or the mournful fall winds howl, or spring has begun to stir the earth, the sunrise arriving ever earlier. You've the sense, or you would if you stopped reading long enough to think it, that there are others out there, alive and awake in the night. Surely, at the hospital downtown. In Johnstown, a steel mill is always thundering along. The Sheetz convenience store a half-mile away is fully staffed, even at 2:00 a.m. Up the road, Eat'n Park produces late-night fries for a few stragglers. Even closer by, your neighbor's up with the baby who won't sleep for more than two hours at a time. But there are others who, like you, are in bed but not asleep, whether because of desires that you don't understand yet, or worries that you don't have yet (lucky girl), or in a few cases, just like you, because there's another page to read.

You'll read on by the light of the moon—poetic but, alas, also eventually damaging. In your midforties, when you're buying reading glasses by the case, you'll remember your mother warning you about just this possibility. But, for now, the moonlight. It's terrible, just terrible, as you'll someday read Emily Webb romantically declare in *Our Town*, which will be your favorite play someday. But tonight, you're here, bathed in the moonlight, snuggled in bed, your eyes inches from the page. It'll be 4:00 a.m. by the time you make it to the end of *Little Women* and fall asleep. You just couldn't bear to pace yourself. You had to keep reading to find out Jo's fate. Someday, you'll learn that her betrothal to that German professor is unpopular, even with the author herself, but for you it's the perfect conclusion and one you expect for yourself.

You're still so young, and these lost hours of sleep can be easily absorbed into your day. You'll be more tired than usual, but no one expects much of you, and you can still cry in the midafternoon for no real reason, half from fatigue, half because the book was over too quickly. No other book will ever be as good again, you think, which isn't true. You can, after school, go to the library with your mom and get another one, which you'll start after dinner, homework, television. Turns out, it's good, too. This time you'll stop reading at 9:00 p.m., fifty pages in, aware, even in your youth, that you cannot pull too many late-nighters in a row.

You'll throw the book on the floor by your bed. You'll always throw the book on the floor by your bed. For the rest of your life, at lights-out, the book will hit the floor, whether you read five pages or fifty. And when adult responsibilities sneak in, first slowly, then quickly over the years and you lie awake at 2:00 a.m., you'll again think of who else might be up nearby, in the factories and hospitals, nurseries and convenience stores of Pittsburgh. You'll know that there are other folks out there picking through the predicaments of their lives. And you'll want an escape, so you'll root around on the bedroom floor for the book and open it, imagining the crack of other book spines all over town, a dozen of you, more, reaching for an evening companion this dark, long night. A few words and you forget your cares—no, you forget yourself altogether—and are brought back to the crisp, straw-shot attention of the nights of your youth. You're still not alone. You still have your book.

TO FINISH A SERIES

I read everything I could get my hands on as a kid—the backs of cereal boxes, the papers on my teachers' desks, even the car manual stashed in the glove compartment on one particularly boring day trip when I had forgotten to bring a book.[4] It was a time of unfettered, unhinged reading, of passing every moment in two lives, one my actual lived existence, and the other wherever my book took me. I miss it. People seem to expect my complete attention so much more often now.

Another lost satisfaction of my youth is reading a series. As a child and teenager, I always seemed to have time to lose myself in a long swath of interconnected stories. I loved the *Little House* books, adored the endless *Anne of Green Gables* procession,[5] and even plodded through the diminishing rewards of the two sequels to *Little Women*. I wound my way

---

4   Have absolutely never forgotten a book again. Always carry at least two at all times.

5   I used to joke that the last one was surely called *Anne of the Cemetery*.

through Frank L. Baum's *The Wizard of Oz* and its myriad sequels. I read most of the *Nancy Drew*s, too, and only skipped the *Hardy Boys* because my grandmother told me that they were mostly about "camping and other boy things."

I know I'm not alone. When I talk to other readers, we often discuss what series we've read. All of the *Harry Potter*s. Tolkien's *Lord of the Rings* books (which is but a trilogy, yet still an enormous undertaking). All of *Goosebumps*, the *Baby-sitters Club* books, *Sweet Valley High*'s shenanigans, or—naughty!— the V. C. Andrews's *Flowers in the Attic* series. Some folks burn through mysteries and have read every Miss Marple or Poirot book. I don't think I know a single fellow Lutheran who didn't make their way through the *Chronicles of Narnia* around age ten. My students loved *Percy Jackson*, the *Divergent* series, and *The Hunger Games*, as well as so many YA fantasy series, I couldn't begin to keep them straight.[6]

Of course, all of those concluded, which I very much appreciate. I fret about series still being written: fingers crossed for all of you reading the *Game of Thrones* books! Good luck, ye Sassenach *Outlander* readers! May those landings, if they ever arrive, stick. My father was a fan of Sue Grafton's series of mysteries starring private detective Kinsey Millhone, which began with *A Is for Alibi* in 1982 and made it to 2017 with *Y Is for Yesterday* before Grafton passed away at seventy-seven. My father died before her, and I'm glad that he didn't know that, to paraphrase Grafton's daughter, the alphabet now ends with *Y*. Somehow, it seems better that the devoted reader exited first.

---

6   So many elves!

Because I grew up before the internet, I never really knew what I was getting into with a book. It often wasn't until I turned to the final page, with its suggestion that I buy the sequel, that I knew I was reading a series at all. I remember the process of gradual realization that there was more story ahead, and then, if I could, racing through the next books ("I will read *The Patchwork Girl of Oz* in twenty-four hours, dang it!"), followed by the realization that I was almost at the end of the line, which slowed me down, stretching out the sweet last moments in the world of the series. And then, when it was over, that was all. The curtain fell. Unless I decided I liked the books enough to read them again, from the top, a compliment reserved for only my very favorites: the *Anne* books and the *Little House* series.

Luxuriating in a series is still a pleasure. My college students have told me that they read those fantasy series they love at a breakneck speed, plot-drunk, desperate to find out what happens, aware that once finished, they can return to the beginning and start again. Perhaps because they've grown up in a world of streaming, their generation seems more willing to make long-term commitments to series, to read and reread, and reread again, living in the world for more than just weeks or months. I rarely felt that way. Or perhaps *Mockingjay* just offers more nuance and reward than *The Patchwork Girl of Oz* did.

By the way, I know I sound down on *The Patchwork Girl of Oz*, but let me assure you, it is a bad book. It's the seventh in the *Oz* series, which would grow to fourteen volumes. The opening involves some incredible narrative heavy lifting to explain why the land of Oz, which was declared to be *entirely* cut off from Earth for *all* time in the prior book, is instead back with another story. The narrator eventually blames it all on "telegraphy." Baum really only wrote it because he was nearly destitute, and while reading, you can almost sense him calculating how much money he will collect once he turns it in.

Series are generally better these days. Frank L. Baum, Agatha Christie, and Louisa May Alcott—a strange dinner party: I'd serve a goose, I think—responded to the pressure from their publishers to produce more content once the first book they created proved popular. I suspect that today's series writers often have already conceived of the multiple books they will craft before the first one is even published, which allows for character arcs and plots that don't require a lot of backtracking and telegraphy. Perhaps that's why the worlds of today's multibook sagas are so rich, while Baum seemed to just add another nearby country full of weirdos with every volume, and *Little Men* is mostly about camping and other boy things.

Still, old or new, genuine outpourings of the spirit or awkward money grabs (or both), series appeal. I think we sometimes forget that reading, even reading solely for pleasure, is real work. Perhaps the physical exertion isn't much, but the demand on our minds is substantial. We have to orient ourselves to the world of the novel (setting, time period, closeness to or distance from our own known lives), as well as the narrator and their attitude toward the world, the characters and the dialogue, which is why I find most books of short stories enervating. But a series usually only asks us to do that heavy lifting at the beginning of the first book, and from then on we can simply wander. It's the equivalent of remembering you have some cooked chicken in the fridge: you can focus on whether to make tacos or noodle soup instead of starting from the broad concept of "What do I feel like eating?"

Yet the pleasure of a series—the intimacy of its world and people—can also chafe. Sometimes you don't want to use up the chicken in the fridge; you want a lamb curry, or three slices of banana bread for dinner. Series can bore with their zombified obligation to keep going, failing to sense when they should have ended. As a teenager, I loved the *Mitford* books about a pastor, his wife, and their small town until I suddenly didn't believe them anymore, like a devoted fan of *Murder, She Wrote* who finally in the fifth season thinks to question how anyone would want to hang out with Jessica Fletcher, given how many people around her have died violently at someone else's hand.

Perhaps the key is for a series' author to revisit but not repeat. I'm sure the *Anne of Green Gables* series also grew because of audience insistence—indeed, during my travels in Prince Edward Island, where the books are set, I saw that the demand for Anne was still vociferous, and I could've come home with T-shirts, mugs, dish towels, and plaques bearing a likeness of the red-haired orphan on them. (I could've also brought home a red wig itself.) But Anne's author, Lucy Maud Montgomery, who, like Baum, also saw her writing as her best chance at financial stability, rose to the challenge of continuing her most famous creation's story in a more organic way. She moved Anne from childhood into an adult life as a teacher, wife, and mother. Anne mourns her losses, lets go of some dreams, endures disappointments, and matures, while still remaining the bright spirit that readers first fell in love with when she was a child. Montgomery's own difficulties are well-documented—she is believed to have died by suicide—and it's clear that she knew the very real troubles that can beset us as we age, if we are lucky enough to avoid them as children. I respect her willingness to allow her fictional creation to mature into a nuanced depiction of human life. She answered her readers' eternal question *Then what happened?* with something deeper than *More of the same.*

Then again, in dismissing *more of the same*, I might be missing the point of a series. Whether each book is a unique adventure or a retread of what sold well last time, the familiarity is the point. It's just not what I'm typically looking to read these days. In fact, I can't recall the last time I made my way through every book in a series, excepting the *Harry Potter*s (more on that later on) and—bit different!—Hilary Mantel's majestic *Wolf Hall* trilogy, each read several years apart from the prior. The fault isn't with series, really, but with me. Instead of enjoying a pleasant ramble over familiar terrain, I get antsy about the idea of devoting that much of my precious free reading time to one world. There are so many books out there! I refuse to be tied down to Tana French's Dublin Murder Squad or the endless titles in the Alexander McCall Smith series, no matter how excellent those series are! Live free, read free!

Still, a part of me does crave a series. Lately, I've been constructing my own, thematic instead of authorial, inspired by what the librarian and author Annie Spence calls "Books That Lead to More Books" in her book, *Dear Fahrenheit 451.*

I began deep in the pandemic, when I suddenly and urgently (and inexplicably) desired to learn more about the ancient people of Britain. Watching the beautiful, melancholy movie *The Dig*, about the discovery of a burial ship and other medieval wonders at Sutton Hoo in southern England, must have started me off. Then, recalling my own travels to Skara Brae, an even older site on the Orkney Islands in Scotland, I longed to go back. Since I couldn't, I suppose I decided to travel in time via book. First, I read the original *The Dig*, by John Preston, then my parents' collection of books and pamphlets from ancient tourist sites in the UK, and before long I found myself deep into Peter Ackroyd's magisterial *Foundation: The History of England from Its Earliest Beginnings to the Tudors*. There was so much I didn't know! I enjoyed reading it such that I resolved to one day make my way through Ackroyd's entire series on the history of England. But not quite yet. Instead, I've chosen to read on thematically, books about tribes and stone circles and pagans, finally ending (for now) with a reread of the adjacent *How the Irish Saved Civilization*, by Thomas Cahill, an all-time favorite.

My imperfect, self-curated thematic series reminded me of the pleasure of reading downward, through the books, of trusting that time invested yields rewards. Breadth and depth are not the same, after all, and I don't want to be the kind of reader who only skims and never delves, so the minute I finish writing this paragraph, I'm going to order up a copy of *Tudors*, the next book in Ackroyd's series. I may not have it in me anymore to read a not-great, fourteen-book sequence of novels about Oz, but I do want to delve more deeply, experiencing, not just remembering, the pleasure of sinking into a series and truly getting to know a world and its chronicler. And perhaps it's time to revisit Anne, too, and see what I think of her in middle age, now that I've arrived there myself. After all, the undisputed pleasure of a series is returning to the familiar, in order to see how you yourself have and have not changed.

CALMED-DOWN CLASSICS OF AMERICAN LITERATURE FOR THE ANXIETY-RIDDEN

The Good-Enough Gatsby

All Heights Are Beautiful Women

Moby, the Bathroom Door Locks Securely, Not to Worry

The Practice Test That Definitely Isn't a Crucible Since the Score Will Not Count

To Mildly Startle a Mockingbird

A Raisin in a Sealed Box in a Cool Kitchen Cupboard Nowhere Near the Expiration Date

Fahrenheit 71 Degrees

Of Cute Animals and Totes Normal People

The Grapes of Poor, but Ultimately Fixable, Life Choices

Gone Girl (But She Left a Note re: When She'll Return)

I'm Going to Tell You Why the Caged Bird Sings: It Will
Not Be a Mystery to You for Much Longer, Deep Breaths

The Beige Letter

1994

BECAUSE WE HAD TO

I hated my assigned reading in middle and high school. *Hated* it. All of it.

I mean, I did it. I read every single book, story, or poem I was assigned throughout my many years of education, up until my senior year in college when I was having far too much fun being what I was sure was a fully-grown adult to read an assigned book about the constellations for my astronomy class.[7] We had to write a paper about said book, and at 8:00 p.m. on the day it was due at midnight, I called home and wailed to my mom[8] about how not even *I* could read an entire book and write a paper on it in just a few hours. She wearily advised me to skim, summarize, and generally stop freaking out about a class I cared so little for that I often referred to it as *Astrology 101*. I did as she advised, and I believe

---

7   Leaving your required science class to the last semester of college = highly mature.

8   Such a fully-grown adult thing to do.

the paper got a B. I strongly suspect the professor paid even less attention to it than I did.

But that was unusual for me. I was and generally am, as my students say, a Try Hard. Even when it truly did not matter, globally or personally, I still did the work I was assigned. My grave marker may someday read *She read every page*.

This characteristic has stayed with me all of my days, which are now spent in academia, aka Try Hard Central. We of the English department did the reading. We *always* did the reading. Somewhere along the line, we enjoyed what we were reading enough to get multiple degrees to allow us to teach others about the reading.

And yet... many of us hated the assigned reading, at least some of it, at least some of the time. Most people do. It's the nature of assigned reading: it must be hated. We, you, I, my colleagues, all of us read because we *had* to, and it just about ruined reading for many of us.

Of course, I'm referring to the assigned reading of English classes, which always bear the brunt of our blame. Our other courses were full of terrible assigned reading, too—apologies if you loved *American History: Our Country, Its Story* more than I did. But we only took the assigned reading personally in English class, for some reason, perhaps because we incorrectly believed that science could never be made interesting, anyway. But novels, stories, poems, they were supposed to be good. For centuries, people had been deriving pleasure from literature, or so we were told. Surely, the works we were assigned in English class had the potential to be enjoyable? At some vague point in the past, people must have read Alfred Noyes's poem, "The

Highwayman," for their own pleasure. It was not originally published in *American Literature: Our Country, Its Stories*, right?

And yet I did not enjoy "The Highwayman," nor *Tess of the D'Urbervilles*, nor "The Legend of Sleepy Hollow," nor pretty much anything that my English textbooks and teachers offered for my reading consumption. Even works that under different circumstances I might have liked—*Mrs. Dalloway* comes to mind—became considerably less interesting to me once they were assigned. I didn't enjoy the few plays we had to read, not even when I got to play John Proctor in *The Crucible*. I also played Elizabeth Proctor. Not a lot of people in my class liked to read aloud.

It's true that I'm a stubborn soul and don't like to be told what to do. But my antipathy for assigned reading went beyond mere crankiness. Like my classmates, like you, I knew what was to come after the reading: worksheets, quizzes, essays, a test. I was good at all of these. I just didn't like them. Not when I knew what reading could be, the kind of reading I did on my own, where the goal was to get lost in the world of a book. I wanted to lose myself in *The Crucible*, truly a fantastically unnerving world. But it's hard to do that when you know you'll be asked to write a five-paragraph essay on what Arthur Miller's purpose in writing it was, using at least three quotes, one from each act of the play.

Nothing kills the experience of reading a good book more than having to answer questions about who the main character is, what his motivation might be, and what the giant glasses symbolize. It's not as if my high-school class—a high-achieving and well-behaved bunch—openly disdained answering those questions. We completed the assignments, but we saw no practical reason for them, not in the present and not for our futures; mostly, I think, we were right. Excluding me and the other three people who became educators, I bet that no one from my class has made much use of the skill of correctly answering worksheet questions over the last thirty years. And I also bet that the four of us have mostly used that skill to... write more worksheet questions. I tend to be skeptical of the idea that every task undertaken in high school should directly tie to a necessary adult competency, but those worksheets also didn't enhance or build our love of reading, or our appreciation for literature, or our understanding of the human condition. They were busywork.

Probably because I had always been a reader, long before I got to school, the worksheets didn't faze me. I kept right on reading anyway, learning to think of making my way through the assigned books as something I had to do, while actual, real reading remained a pleasure. But many of my classmates just abandoned reading altogether, understandably underwhelmed by the way school turned it into a fact-finding mission. Many of my students tell me that's what they've done, too. They arrive in my class eager to learn to write books even though they no longer like to read them (or so they think). At best, they, like me, have tacitly learned to split their reading into the categories of Assigned Reading and Reading I Actually Enjoy. At worst, they don't read much of anything at all.

I want them to read more.

So what do I do? I assign reading.

It really is the great conundrum of my teaching life, an irony I rue every day of the semester: I hated assigned reading, everyone I knew (and know) hated (hates) assigned reading, and now I get paid to assign reading. O Irony! If sixteen-year-old Shannon, head bent wearily over Woolf's *Mrs. Dalloway*, could see forty-eight-year-old Shannon now, adding a little Woolf to her syllabus! Life comes at you fast.

But the truth is that for all my bluster above, I have come to see the point of assigned reading. Not the worksheets, not the quizzes—neither of which I ever use in my classroom now—but the direct prompt to engage with the works themselves. Take John Steinbeck's *The Grapes of Wrath*. It's a strange, sad, beautiful book, one that I think about surprisingly often. Being forced to read it in my sophomore year of high school introduced me to and gave me a way to think about American poverty, American striving, and the narrative uses of dialect for good or ill. I cannot say I liked the book— my mom and brother can still recollect my specific and bitter complaints about that dialect—but, on some level, I enjoyed it. It stayed with me. I would never have read it on my own, not in a million years, and perhaps it wasn't the best possible choice for a fourteen-year-old girl in Western Pennsylvania who got skittish around all discussion of boobs... but ultimately I'm very glad I did read it. I want such experiences for my students, that broadening of their minds, that glimpse into other times and lives, like and unlike theirs. And the strange beauty of the writing.

In a perfect world, perhaps, I would have come to *The Grapes of Wrath* on my own, just as my students would ideally pick up *Little Fires Everywhere* during their downtime rather than arriving at it through my syllabus. But this is not a perfect world, Candy Crush has too many levels to ever be conquered, and I know that I myself haven't gotten around to reading many worthy books without being assigned them.

So now, part of my work with my creative writing students is to fold the categories of Assigned Reading and Reading I Actually Enjoy back together. What I try to do is assign well-written books and provide my students help in understanding them. This seems tragically basic, but the idea that books ought to be enjoyable is not at all pervasive in academia, alas. I insist on it, though; everything we read has to have the possibility of giving a reader pleasure.[9] I wish I could share with you a photo of my students looking skeptical when I tell them that they will like the books I've assigned. At the outset they do *not* think so. But eventually, they (mostly) do.

Community helps. In a way, the community is another assignment, as my students ended up with each other in my class through no fault or merit of their own. But when I assign a book, we're all in it together. Such camaraderie was often missing from my high-school classes, unless you count the kinship of furtively passing around pirated photocopies of CliffsNotes about *Wuthering Heights*. In my class, I try to to give us room to talk about the books, to unpack them as a group. I hope that this might encourage them to want to read more deeply and broadly than they have thus far.

I won't deny that I'm partly relying on peer pressure here, the Teacher's Little Helper that we aren't supposed to admit to activating; but more, I'm hoping that the communal aspects of reading will win the class over, too. Reading is a solitary

---

9   Pleasure comes in many forms—this is starting to sound like an adult bookstore ad—so fear not, my assigned reading is not always comfy or cheery. In fact, most of the time, it decidedly isn't.

pursuit, by nature, but the pleasure of discussing what one has read is deeply collective, the reason why we seek out book clubs, press a novel we enjoyed into a friend's hands, and jet to review sites to warn others away from (or beckon them into) a book. All sorts of wonderful things happen when my students talk about the books we're reading together: they realize that they were not the only person who didn't understand chapter 3; they learn which of their classmates has the most insightful ideas; they mirror the pleasures and sorrows of the narrative to each other; and, I dearly hope, they make friends with their fellow readers. Sometimes, we even learn a little bit about writing!

To my surprise, bringing students back to enjoying assigned reading is a true pleasure of the job. So many students tell me that they most likely will not be able to get through our assigned reading on time. I smile, knowing that in a week or two, they'll be telling me they raced through all of *Gone Girl* in a day. It's a delight to allow them such an experience. To assign it, really. No quizzes or worksheets or essays about themes loom. My only request is that they come to class ready to discuss together just what they think of the book and the experience of reading it.[10]

As much as I love the thanks, I don't deserve it. I mean, it's not as if I wrote *Gone Girl* or discovered and brought it to international attention. All I've really done is release my students from the pointless rigor of those assignments we all hated while prioritizing and gently shoving them toward books that are, well, good, and not just canon, which I admit

---

10 Don't worry—they've had main themes and literary elements so ingrained in them that we always end up talking about those, too.

is a luxury I have because I teach contemporary fiction. I'm glad I catch some students before they sink completely out of reading. Life is so much better with books than without.

But what about those of us who do not want to amass college credits in order to heal our old assigned-reading wounds? If we read because we had to, what do we do now that we want to be someone who reads because they like to?

These are really good questions, so let me say first that if you do not want to assign yourself any reading at all, that's fine by me. Read whatever you like, books about railroads or by Real Housewives, romances set in quaint New England towns in the fall, mysteries in which Queen Elizabeth II somehow stops a murder in between the whole being-queen thing. Tom Clancy. Danielle Steele. Whatever. Just keep reading.

But if I were to make a tiny argument for assigned reading, it's just this: as I discovered with *The Grapes of Wrath*, I very rarely can accurately predict what I'll get out of a book—pleasure, joy, education, insight, disgust, boredom—until I actually read it. There have been so many times when I've so-called assigned myself a book because I felt I *should* read it and then ended up enjoying the writing itself, on its own merits. Sally Rooney's first novel, *Conversations with Friends*, comes to mind. I picked it up as a logical assignment of the I Should Read This variety. I'm Irish by heritage, I teach contemporary-fiction writing to Gen Z students, and Rooney is one of our finest modern, Irish, Gen Z-ish, contemporary-fiction writers. I mean no insult to her when I say that at no

point before beginning the book did I think, "Oohhh, am I
gonna love this one!" But once I did start it, of course I did
love it. Neil Gaiman's *The Ocean at the End of the Lane* also
comes to mind. I assigned it to myself because I had never
read any Gaiman and ended up enjoying it so much that I
now teach it, an assignment I'm pretty sure will give most of
my students pleasure, too. You'll likely confront similar sur-
prises when you assign yourself a book.

I also think we underestimate just how weird—unexpected,
unusual—a lot of famous books are. A long time spent in the
public consciousness can sand down a book's rough edges.
But isn't it a little surprising that *Gatsby* has a first-person narrator? We've come to expect that famous books have a more
omniscient narrative stance, but *Gatsby* is rooted in Nick's
perspective alone. And it's odd that *Wuthering Heights* has,
like, five beginnings. How strange for *Dracula* to be an epistolary novel, of all things. It's pretty fun to go back into those
supposedly staid classics and find all of that out. So many of
them were unconventional and unique in voice and scope, a
lovely reminder that the conventional, traditional, and staid
is not necessarily what lasts.

All right, then. If you want to give assigned reading a go,
where to begin? Well, you could go back to the books you
were ordered to read in high school and revisit them with
fresh eyes. My best friend, Andrew, makes it a point to occasionally reread a classic.[11] I don't believe he's found any
new firm favorites, but he has said things like, "So I get the

---

11 He abandoned *The Grapes of Wrath* in high school because, after reading
    the first chapter, he thought it was about a turtle.

chapters about the whale now," so I think he's glad he does this. I have another friend who returned to Dickens, having hated *A Tale of Two Cities* in high school, and loved him so much he ended up getting a PhD with a Dickensian thesis.[12] And there are plenty of people in the world who returned to their assigned reading by actually reading the book for the first time, having relied on CliffsNotes or SparkNotes or Wikipedia or just bullshittery the first time through. I can't say for sure that you'll love the books once you actually read them, but even a few years of lived life will likely have made you more amenable to them. I mean, the boobs stuff of *The Grapes of Wrath* is very small potatoes to me now. Anyway, give them another try. The takeaway might only be *Okay, that was not as bad as I thought*, but that might be enough to heal. Remember: no worksheets this time around. And there's always another book on the horizon.

Or perhaps you're more like me, which is to say that you've never gone back to your high-school reading list. I've always held that there were too many books out there for me to re-read one I already know I don't like. If you hated *Romeo and Juliet*, you do not need to drag yourself through fair Verona now, after working, and doing the dishes, and also taking the garbage out because it's Tuesday. Frankly, you do not want to read about two hormonal teenagers who never had to take the garbage out or even remember that it's Tuesday at all. Skip *R & J*. You are allowed to watch *Emily in Paris* instead. Or perhaps a trip to Italy, full of ardor and romance and violence and really poor decision-making is just what you need, after

---

12   What a Try Hard.

all. You never know. You'll at least be proud of yourself for sticking to your assignment.[13]

Or it might be best to start fresh, anyway. How about a book you might have been assigned but were not? You might enjoy it, or get something out of it, or just be glad you no longer have to fake-nod your way through conversations about Mary Shelley's *Frankenstein*, since you have now actually read it.

As a former high-school teacher who's fully aware books get taught for all kinds of reasons, I'm very wary of the commonly held belief that *the classics are the classics for a reason*. The real reason *Ethan Frome* is taught is because it's short and there are about five billion copies available in our nation's school book rooms. But to assign yourself some reading is an opportunity to avail yourself of the better elements of classic literature: the beauty of the prose in *I Know Why the Caged Bird Sings*, the unique insights of the author in *Narrative of the Life of Frederick Douglass*, or, as with *Beowulf*, a glimpse of the impact the story has made throughout the years, decades, or centuries it has been in our culture. It may be worth your time. Remember, no worksheets, no quizzes, no busywork. Just you and a book that you're smart enough to appreciate and canny enough to put down if it's not for you, assigned or not. Every book can be a Book You Actually Enjoy, I promise.

---

13 Although, as you'll read later on, you might prefer an audiobook for that one.

TO BREAK THE RULES

On most days, if you encountered me, you'd see an acceptably alert woman in her late forties, dressed in jeans, a black shirt, and Danskos. My reading glasses are on my head, my hair is in a messy bun, and I'm probably holding forth about the impossibility of finding a parking spot on campus while spilling cookie crumbs down my shirt. Just a standard-issue twenty-first century English professor, (hopefully) played by Tina Fey in the cinematic version of my life. That's me.

But on the inside, I have an alter ego who looks more like Cate Blanchett in the *Lord of the Rings* movies: ethereal, soft-lit, and wearing gauzy, neutral-colored clothes. She is calm but focused and hasn't had a cookie in months. Her name is… Shanogas. As Enya's music swirls around her, she smiles beatifically. Come closer, because the mysterious, attractive, and surprisingly nice-smelling Shanogas has a message for you: she wants you to be *free*.

Wait. Clarification: not, like, the naked and tripping kind

of free. Shanogas doesn't care much about that side of your life, so long as she doesn't have to see it. No, Shanogas wants you to be free *as a reader*. She wants you to read whatever you want, whenever you like, however you prefer, wherever you choose. She definitely does not want you to begrudgingly put away *Book Lovers* by Emily Henry and open up Doris Kearns Goodwin's *Team of Rivals* just to impress her. But she also doesn't want you to hide *Team of Rivals* if you were enjoying it.

You see, for many a long year (Decade? Century? Hard to tell how old Shanogas is, her skin is *very* good), she has been watching humanity fumble around as readers, keeping her eye particularly on the undergrads of Western Pennsylvaniashire. It's not going great. A lot of people who would be happier if they were reading more books are actually reading less. This is mostly the fault of cell phones. Shanogas would journey to the Mountain of Fire and throw all cell phones into its molten core except that she has an amazing streak on Duolingo herself that she doesn't want to break, *malheureusement*.

But it's not *all* the fault of cell phones. There are other villains, holding people back from being readers. Shanogas, smiling benevolently but with a *soupçon* of irritation in her eyes, knows what has happened: there are simply too many rules about reading. She's not quite sure where such rules have come from, although well-meaning parents, teachers, and librarians are probably at least partially to blame. Worse, the higher up the ladder of being a Good Reader she sees people go, the more rules they seem to have internalized. (Shanogas doesn't really understand internalization, since her every emotion is clear to her at all times, but she gets the gist.)

What kind of rules does Shanogas sense you're trying to

follow, causing her grief? Why, the rules of the Good Reader.
No one can entirely escape them. She's seen the most unlikely
people fall for them, including the Uber driver who—uh, the
winged chariot driver who escorted Shanogas home from
Homedepotshire, and who commented unkindly about the
Tina Brown book Shanogas had in her bag. So many people
have somehow come to believe that there are correct ways to
read and to be a Good Reader.

To wit:

Good Readers read fast.

Good Readers never need to reread because they immediately understand every word they've read, no nuance missed.

If a Good Reader happens upon a word they do not understand (ye gods!), they immediately stop reading, look up the
word in the dictionary, memorize the definition, and return
to the book. They never assume that not quite knowing one
word isn't that big a deal. They also never forget the meaning of that word again.

Good Readers read the book before watching the movie
adaptation. They also always find the book superior.

Good Readers read at their grade level and never look up
plot summaries on Wikipedia. Further, Good Readers don't
need SparkNotes (or, back in ancient times, when Shanogas
was but a young elf princess, CliffsNotes). Good Readers instinctively understand main themes and can articulate them
in five-paragraph essays.

Those are just the *academic* Good Reader beliefs Shanogas has encountered. There are many, many more of them
outside the classroom. Good Readers don't read audiobooks,
or romances, or YA, or mysteries, or erotica. Good Readers

don't read horror, or if they do, they only read Stephen King's horror, and if they read those, then only the ones deemed Good, like *The Stand*.[14] Good Readers don't read Those Authors, You Know Which Ones We Mean. Good Readers don't enjoy rereading a Louis L'Amour paperback now and then. They certainly never pick up a Judy Blume classic from their own childhood, and—heavens, no!—they don't reread *Ramona and Beezus* on a particularly bad day. Good Readers buy their kids, niblings, or godkids earnest books for children about racism and LGBTQ+ issues, never books with titles that have the word *poop* in them.

A Good Reader would never use an e-book reader. They always try to buy books brand-new, or only from used bookstores, or only in first editions, or they don't buy them at all but take them out of libraries. Good Readers only hold onto books that spark joy, and they read the books they have on the home shelf before buying more, or they allow themselves to buy whatever books they'd like, so long as they're from local bookstores. They don't reread, always finish, and never skim. If a Good Reader finds a popular or well-reviewed book boring, the problem, they know, is with them.

Shanogas is already tired from this list of rules and is thinking about maybe just ordering a pizza this evening instead of cooking her usual dinner of twigs and ferns. But as she pulls out her phone, she remembers there are even more rules, about whether a Good Reader can have their phone out when they're making their way through a book, and whether they're

---

14   But a real Good Reader has only ever read King's *On Writing*.

allowed to declare a book DNF[15] at less than twenty pages in, and whether they should or should not listen to music while they read.

Shanogas seriously just wants to lie down now, a cool cloth dipped in the Elysian waters on her still-somehow-unwrinkled brow, but she then recalls that there's even an entire subset of rules that are about marking a place in a book. Good Readers don't bend corners, or break the spine, or make notes in anything but very light pencil. Good Readers don't leave books open and facedown. Good Readers should never... wait. Shanogas? Are you crying?

Yes, she surely is, but tears of frustration. In her elvish language—she is sorry it is not available on Duolingo, as it's quite lovely, silvery and tinkling, but anyway—Shanogas wants to know, who the bejeezus has time for all this nit-picking about what a Good Reader is and does? Humanity, she's almost screaming now—although it just sounds like unusually virulent wind chimes on the breeze—don't you see that perhaps at one time some of these rules came from good intentions but they have calcified into absurdity? They are ridiculous!

At this point, Shanogas stops yelling but crosses her graceful arms in irritation. The problem, she mutters, is that we don't laugh at these rules. We believe them, or some of them, anyway, these hurdles to reading more, buried so deep in our consciousness that we don't even notice that we are stumbling over them time and time again.

Worse, the rules about how to read trickle down (or up, whatever, Shanogas doesn't have time for human science)

---

15 *Did Not Finish*

into what we choose to read. Already cowed by the number of rules about reading, we meekly buy into every publishing company's marketing campaign. Before we know it, we've stumbled into new rules: John le Carré novels are for men, Emma Straub novels are for women, literary fiction is for people who don't laugh, books that are funny are for people who don't think. Maya Angelou is for Black readers, Elizabeth Strout is for your grandmother's book club, and no one is actually going to read, let alone enjoy, that book about depression by Andrew Solomon, it's just for show. Of course, a second's thought makes us realize that these are nonsensical rules. All of these writers and all of their books have merit for whoever wants to read them.

Shanogas sighs. Reading has brought her so much joy, taught her so many things, provided such succor, even going back to when she was just a tiny elf-sprite with a battered copy of *The House at Pooh Corner*, that she cannot stand it when other people are kept from reading a book by anything but their own interest. She is extremely vexed. It's possible she might need to eat a hot fudge sundae, putting her ethereal wardrobe at extreme risk because Shanogas, for all of her beauty, light, and grace, is a messy eater.

But, thankfully, as she starts digging around in the cupboard to see if she still has some sprinkles, she's pretty sure she has some rainbow ones but she'd prefer the chocolate, something clicks for Shanogas. She realizes that all of the rules are actually *preferences*. Preferences are not rules. Everyone gets to have their own preferences, and no one's preferences, not even the preferences of Tom Hankolas, serve everyone else!

Shanogas looks directly at the camera and smirks. Hey, y'all, she says, it's extremely unlikely that any of us will become so famous that our home library will be donated to the Smithsonian, like Julia Child's kitchen, so why would it possibly matter that we sometimes use a pen to make notes in books we own? Go for it. What's more, bend the corners sometimes! Shanogas doesn't always look up words! She skims! There are volumes in the Shanogas home library that she will not read, even if she lives to the expected elf queen age of nine hundred! Oh, and she went through a period of reading a lot of Danielle Steele as a teenager, and those books were page-turners, as it turns out! Those were and are and will be her preferences, and preferences are fine! It was fine, all along! It still is fine! It's all fine!

Picture a ball of light emanating from but yet also surrounding Shanogas. Her eyes flash. She raises her scepter, which is topped by a golden bookmark. In her deepest voice, like Cate Blanchett in *Elizabeth* when she's on a horse and leading her soldiers into battle, she proclaims, "Read what you want, how you want!"

She can almost hear the raised voices of millions respond, "We will, we shall, and we'll stop reading if we don't like the book!"

Shanogas glows with pleasure, a small but satisfied smile on her perfect face. You almost don't notice the peanut butter smeared across her tunic and onto the book cover. What can she say? Shanogas prefers to snack while she reads.

SIGNS YOU MAY BE A FEMALE CHARACTER IN A WORK OF HISTORICAL FICTION

Your name is Sarah.

A stranger has walked up to you, explained how a system of transportation works, and left before you could further converse with him.

You call pancakes *flapjacks*, *hoecakes*, *griddle bibs*, or anything other than *pancakes*.

You have a propensity for turning on the radio just as some world-changing news is reported. Also, you still listen to the radio.

Your best friend is a horse.

People often tell you not to be afraid of things, including icy ponds, beauty parlors, muskets, ferrets, the dark, and hot stew. Invariably, you have to interact with this thing before too long.

You are tired of the way you must dress every day, which involves seventeen layers, one of which itches.

Handsome men make you swoon. No one else is concerned about the swooning, which is not a thing that twenty-first century people actually do.

Your mother is either dead or dead set on getting you married as quickly as possible.

Men have compared you to an animal (a cow, a mule, a fox), and you did not tweet your outrage about it because you have never heard of Twitter.

You often have conversations in which predictions are made that will prove to be ironic: "I think that William Henry Harrison, the ninth and current president of the United States, looks very well this cold Inauguration Day and will likely serve out two, or more, full terms!"

You carry, fling, wear, shake, tuck, bite, wave, flap, beckon with, hide, show off, remove, and fan yourself with your gloves.

You have a younger brother named Jimmy, Bobby, Billy, or Davy, and he is a scamp.

You have met Mark Twain at the very moment you needed to make a pivotal, life-changing decision. He was gruff but charming, laughing but wise. His eyes twinkled.

You currently hate the man you will end up marrying. He most likely works with your father. This dislike started in elementary school when he teased you about your (adorable and now entirely vanished) lisp. You put him in his place by winning the spelling bee.

Your favorite song is the only one anyone remembers from your time period.

You are so beautiful naturally you do not need makeup, which is convenient because it's hard to research makeup.

Also, your hair is naturally gorgeous and requires no product. You are most likely a redhead. If not, you have *glints of fiery red* in your brown hair.

You have a maid who either scolds you, or adores you, or both. You have never shown the slightest interest in exploring her interior life. Neither has she.

You stop by a general store at least once a week. You are very interested in the calicos.

You have a pony, a jalopy, or a Mustang convertible your brother fixed up for you.

You eagerly await the mail.

You think you do not like dancing until the guy who works for your dad forces you to dance. Then it turns out that you love it. It is high-spirited fun! Your makeup-free face glows beautifully. As the guy who works for your dad pulls you in for a closemouthed yet passionate kiss, you glimpse Mark Twain nodding approvingly before he slips out the door into the night.

TO LEARN ABOUT
(AND FROM) THE PAST

My late father was born with extreme wanderlust. He wanted to go everywhere and see everything; traveling truly was a necessity for him. As a young dad, he loved to pack up the entire family for long road trips around America, taking us to Yellowstone, Yosemite, Las Vegas, Cape Cod, and the Great Smokey Mountains. Even in his later years, when he could not travel as easily, he was always up for driving a couple of towns over for dinner. The act of being on the road, of going somewhere definite, was his panacea.

After my brother and I grew up, my parents began to travel internationally, but before that, every summer of our youth involved a two-to-four-week trip driving around the U.S. By the time I graduated high school, I had been to every mainland state except Florida, ignored because it was deemed too popular, although some members of the family think that we cut across the upper-left corner once on our way to Mississippi.[16] Those trips were a lot of different things all at once: exhausting, bonding, exhilarating, dull, aggravating, educational, and beautiful. As much as I enjoyed the stops we made, what I really loved was the traveling itself. In the back seat, Justin and I invented games and songs and stupid conflicts with each other. We watched the country go by, ate a lot of Goldfish crackers, fell asleep staring out the window at the stars (we never seemed to make it to our hotel before 10:00 p.m., not when there was so much to see), and collected innumerable postcards, National Park Passport stamps, and brochures, turning the back seat into a seething pile of papers. Adding to the clutter were the twenty or so library books around my seat. Justin had a dozen, too. Over the course of the trip, we made our way through all of them. It was great.

Of course, we were traveling in the '80s and '90s, long before the days of the supposedly family-oriented trips of today, in which children are apparently taken to special destinations to go on special activities arranged specifically for their pleasure. I get cranky about that. When my friends with kids worry aloud about whether their children will be properly entertained by the fifteen hundred different available activities on the kid-friendly cruise they've booked, I recollect us driving across Iowa with only the Corn Palace to look forward to,[17] expected to entertain ourselves for hours without phones or DVD players. If I am beginning to sound like Walter Matthau here, I apologize. I'm just jealous, I think. My friends' kids go to amusement parks for a week; Justin and I

---

16   I still have never been to Florida, although I've made it to Hawaii and Alaska (twice).

17   And we didn't even go inside the Corn Palace. Cost too much.

were marched around every state capitol, through any nearby historical fort, and in and out of the Hoover Dam (twice).

So it especially stands out in my memory when we went to an attraction that was actually chosen for us. That's why I remember all of the Hard Rock Cafés (for me) and comic-book shops (for Justin) we stopped at. It's also why I vividly remember stopping to see one of the places where Laura Ingalls Wilder had lived.

Entire books have been written about how influential the *Little House on the Prairie* series was to my generation of Gen X white girls, we who were double-teamed by the television show, which ran from 1974 to 1983, and the books, which began with the publication of *Little House in the Big Woods* in 1932. When I was four or five, Mum-mum gave me the entire series, doling them out one at a time, all the way through *The First Four Years*,[18] and I read them sequentially. After that, I dipped back into them constantly, always willing to go back to the Little Houses, to Ma and Pa Ingalls, and Mary and Laura and baby Carrie. My favorite of the series was *Farmer Boy*, the only book in the series not actually about Laura. Instead she writes about her husband's childhood, which glows off the page, so warm and comfortable does it seem.

The other *Little House* books didn't have quite the same self-satisfied feeling, focusing as they did on Wilder's loving but peripatetic childhood. In each book, she writes about a home she shares with her family, beginning in Wisconsin when she is five and traveling through the wild Midwest and Western

---

18 There are more books by Laura's daughter, Rose Wilder, but they arrived after my childhood so I don't count them.

territories until she marries at eighteen in *These Happy Golden Years*. Although there are wonderful scenes of simple holidays, community dances, and delicious food, Wilder's books are also full of toil, danger, and disease, the stuff of the pioneer life.

Yet I related to them. For one thing, the Ingallses seem to be at the mercy of Pa's wanderlust, and I've already mentioned how we four Reeds roamed the U.S. because my dad wanted, always, to see more. But the even stronger connection came through our beloved Mum-mum, our mom's mother, the giver of the *Little House* books, who was a pioneer woman herself, in her own way. She lived in a little house on the edge of the woods on a mountain in Central Pennsylvania, and she sewed, embroidered, crocheted, and gardened. She made many of my clothes, which were mostly skirts and dresses. Until I was in middle school, she had a party-line telephone (that's a line shared betwixt neighbors, with each household having a distinct ring).[19] There was just a hint of the 1800s about her, and she tried to pass many of her skills on to me, although I was not always a natural. When I read about Laura's disdain for having her sewing critiqued by Ma, I could relate.

Perhaps because I connected to Laura's frustrations over getting her stitches straight and small, I completely missed the issues of class and poverty just visible underneath the surface of the *Little House* books, the way the Ingallses were almost always on the edge of abject poverty. When I imagined the characters, I mostly pictured the actors from the TV show. It

19 The idea was that you would only pick up when you heard your ring, which obviously was not adhered to, so everyone on that mountain knew everyone else's business.

was not so much that I didn't understand that there had been
a real Laura, just that I imagined her to have been like the
Laura I knew, the one played by Melissa Gilbert with faintly
1970s makeup and hair. I figured that she spent her days like
I did at my grandmother's, snug and warm and well-fed and
slightly frustrated by her sewing needle.

I fondly, if vaguely, remember the Laura Ingalls Wilder
Museum in Walnut Grove, Minnesota, but what I really recollect about that visit was what Google Maps now lists as "the
Original Site of the Ingalls Family Dugout" down the road.
Dad, a completist, would have insisted that we go there even
if I hadn't wanted to, but I did. It was a fact-finding mission. I'd always been faintly puzzled by the idea of a dugout, featured in the fourth book, *On the Banks of Plum Creek*.
Wilder's narrator made it sound as if the family lived in a hole
in the ground, but I knew that could not possibly be correct.
People lived in *houses*. The series was about the Little *Houses*
of Laura's life. It was impossible to imagine Melissa Gilbert
living in a muddy hovel, after all.

When we pulled in at the original site of the Ingalls family dugout and got out of the car, I was still searching for
the *Hobbit*-sian house illustrator Garth Williams pictured on
the cover of *On the Banks of Plum Creek*, as we walked over
to the riverbank. The illustration is of a free-spirited, loose-
haired, suspiciously clean Laura frolicking on the ground over
her mother's head as the older woman performs some sort
of household task inside what appears to be a cozy earthen
home. But Williams's fantasia bore no resemblance to what
we were staring at. Without the sign, we wouldn't have found
it. It wasn't even a hole, really, just a sort of depression. Ret-

rospectively, I grasp that the hole must have been closed up over the years. The slump I could barely locate without my dad's help must have once offered access to an earthen room large enough to offer shelter and bed pallets. But all I could picture were moles, tunneling around in the earth.

"Ugh, those poor people," my mom said. Dad nodded in agreement, both of them staring at the slump, where all five Ingallses must have lived.

Trying to make this make sense, I suddenly remembered the plot of the book: the first thing Pa does when his family arrives at Plum Creek (having left behind their little house on the prairie) is trade for two horses, horses being more important than not living in a hole in the ground. Then, he buys lumber and wheat seed on credit (also more important than vacating the hole for a house) in hopes that a good crop will allow him to pay this back. Later in the book, a locust swarm destroys Pa's wheat crop *and* next year's crop, then Pa ends up having to walk hundreds of miles to work and then almost dies in a blizzard. Exactly 0 percent of the book was cozy, now that I stopped to think about it. In short: these people had a lot of problems, living in a hole in the ground was only one of them, and nobody was eating Mum-mum's cookies or snuggling under Mum-mum's warm quilts in the tidy, perfectly clean, upstairs (heated) bedroom.

The Ingallses, I realized, were very, very poor.

So much more of the books snapped into place for me, staring at that slump. I understood Ma's constant undercurrent of fear and worry. I better grasped why Laura and Mary, who must have been bedraggled and dirty, were targets of Nellie's cruel bullying. I fully felt the precariousness of their lives. My family of four was carting more things on our three-week vacation than the Ingallses had owned in Plum Creek, and we had a whole house of stuff to return to, not to mention running water and electricity. They only had each other.

Context. That's what I got out of that visit. A deeper understanding of the world of the work I was reading and the forces that shaped it. Joining my father's travels provided more context for me over the years. Once we visited rural, remote Prince Edward Island, I better understood another favorite series from my childhood, the *Anne of Green Gables* books. I had known that Anne was an orphan, but until I saw the beautiful but isolated world of PEI, I didn't understand how needed her labor was on her adopted parents' farm (even if she wasn't the boy that they had asked for). When Marilla yelled at her for abandoning her work, and when Matthew allowed her to sneak away, I understood that both Marilla's frustration and Matthew's indulgence ran deeper than I had previously grasped.

In Bath, England, we saw the fancy homes and insularity of the small city, the backdrop for Jane Austen's shenanigans in *Pride and Prejudice* and *Northanger Abbey*. The houses stood so close together, I could finally comprehend how gossip and innuendo traveled at warp speed without telephones. The precise beauty of the town showed me how much the people of Edwardian England valued appearances, and I understood how quickly propriety could be offended.

In Dublin, we walked in the parks and squares, and I realized how sociable the city was. At every shop I stopped in, even the grocer's, I was asked about my heritage down to the

county my family might have hailed from, and then given a
cheerful lecture on where my interlocutor's American relatives
lived.[20] James Joyce's "The Dead" could only take place there.

Of course, context is not just location. Over the years, I've
come to enjoy learning about authors' upbringings, the worlds
they published into, and other contextual details that help me
understand books better. As I've become a writer myself, I've
grown more interested in the various ways writers live out
their lives. I carry with me the context that each work I read
was written by a person who loved, wept, pooped, and slept.
All writers were once children who had to grow up in a particular place and time, who eventually wrote from that background. It's certainly possible to appreciate a work without
having any context for it, but my experience on the banks of
Plum Creek keeps teaching me that to truly understand and
appreciate a work, a little context helps a great deal.

Of course, I cannot take my students to centuries past, let
alone to most of the places where the books we read together
are set. For all that I like to poke fun at my father's idea of a
vacation (did I mention that we also visited all nearby college
campuses?), I'm so grateful for the trips he planned for us, and
I'm sorry I can't recreate them for my classes. But we have
something now the Reed family of the 1980s did not: the
internet. It's chock-full of much crapola, I know, but also of
many wonders. When teaching "The Dead," recently, I may
not have been able to pack us all off to Dublin, but I could
show them around the streets of the city online. We found
historical photos, and read a Wikipedia article about James

20   (Always San Diego or Boston.)

Joyce. We even listened to an audio clip of the city recorded not long after the story was published, the clatter of horses' hooves mingling with the squawk of seagulls.

Was any of this strictly necessary? No. Joyce's work, like Wilder's, glimmers with humanity even without the context. It's so thoroughly of its time that it teaches us even without the trips, without Wikipedia, without audio of Dublin Bay. Context offers ways in (and, perhaps, ways out) of these stories, but the stories are the actual point. When they're good, they reveal us back to ourselves. When they're great, we gasp with recognition, across the centuries: those people, we think, they're like we are now.

FOR LOVE

I caught my coteacher, Marie, red-handed.

She must have hoped I wouldn't see her. Our class of pre-schoolers napped on their little sleep pads, and I was assigned to sit with them, still and quiet in the dark, ready with an emergency back rub or lullaby.

But for once, they'd all fallen asleep, so when I heard Marie loudly rustling around in the other room, the one with our toys and books and art supplies, I popped my head out the door to shush her. That's when I caught her, shoving a flat, squarish book onto a shelf high above the kids' eye level.

"Marie!" I exclaimed. "What are you doing?"

She whipped around to face me, already shaking her head. "I can't do it," she said, tears forming. "I just cannot read *Old MacDonald Had a Farm* to them even one more time."

It was March, the grayest of Western Pennsylvania's months. All of us, students and teachers, were stir-crazy, desperate to get outside for recess again. We were tired of everything:

school, activities, gym time, each other, everything except napping and snack time. On that particular day, the day Marie broke bad, it was sleeting. We'd begun to question whether we'd make it to April.

Appalled as I was, I knew she was on to something. The kids had fixated on that particular book, which was really just the lyrics to the song "Old MacDonald Had a Farm" spread across the pages. Each line was accompanied by drawings of farm animals. The artistry was dubious. One creature looked like the result of a pig and a sheep getting a little too friendly, if you know what I mean. It was the kind of detail you wouldn't notice on the first, or even the fifth read-through, but by the twelfth, you started to think that this sheep/pig might haunt your sleep. By the twenty-fifth read, it had.

"But they love that book," I said.

"They won't let us sing it!" Marie hissed.

Also true. Our students typically adored singing, particularly "Old MacDonald Had a Farm." But for some reason, they never wanted to sing that song while reading the book. They deeply believed at some core, three-year-old level, that the book should not be sung but *read*, preferably without any discernable rhythm. In a flat, affectless voice. Even the E-I-E-I-Os. They complained and cried if we failed at this. If you have ever met a toddler, you understand their vehemence.

"It's too hard," Marie said, and I knew what she meant. Please try to recite even one E-I-E-I-O without rhythm. Go as slowly as you like. I'll wait while you lose your mind.

As I sighed, Marie gestured at our overflowing bookshelf, a reminder that we had a million other picture books that we could read with the class: books of higher quality, books

that were funnier, books that taught more meaningful concepts, books about grief and new siblings and parents getting
divorced. We had a book about rocks that was as boring as
hell, but the kids loved it. We had books with ducks, cows,
and dogs, all identifiably not mutant. We had books for which
we had cassette tapes, allowing us all to happily sing along
while reading those books together (this was allowed by the
children, for reasons unknown). We had giant books, two feet
tall. We had *Pat the Bunny*, which they actually agreed to carefully pass around so that every one of them got to touch each
page. (Reading *Pat the Bunny* took at least thirty minutes.)
We had a vast library, in other words, plenty of good books,
which is what Marie's gesture said. Her expression begged
me to agree that there was absolutely no reason to revisit *Old
MacDonald Had a Farm* ever again.

I looked back into my room, where several children were
sleeping facedown, their noses smooshed into the carpet. A
few were drooling. They weren't geniuses, I reminded myself. We'd be able to pull this off. Probably.

I gave Marie a nod of agreement, just as a child called out
for me. Smiling beatifically, Marie hurriedly finished hiding
Old MacDonald Had a Farm on the shelf. I returned to work.

After the students got up from their nap (twenty minutes),
and after toileting and handwashing (a lifetime), we settled
down on the rug for Storytime. At first, things went well.
Marie had chosen *Chicka Chicka Boom Boom*, playing the cassette of the book so we could all sing along.

*"A told B! And B told C! I'll meet you at the top of the coco-
nut tree!"* we bellowed, thrilled to be young, well-rested, and

singing at the top of our lungs. We made it all the way to the end, giggling. D is such a character!

And then Marie made her first mistake. It was a big one.

"What should we read next?" she asked, as if *The Monster at the End of the Book* and *Farmer Duck* weren't right there on the shelf behind her, waiting.

I must have gasped at her stupidity in asking an open-ended question, because her eyes widened and she started babbling while flailing one arm behind her, trying to grab a book before anyone answered, "Or let's, just, uh, *Farmer Duck*, shall we, what a great, ducks as farmers, uh…"

But it was too late. Someone, probably Tyler, because it was almost always Tyler, said, "Let's read *Old MacDonald Had a Farm*!"

A heavy silence fell. They suspect nothing, I told myself. Remember, they were drooling into the carpet!

But I couldn't deny the feeling of menace in the air. Marie and I exchanged glances, hers apologetic and fearful. I knew it was all up to me.

"I love *Farmer Duck*," I said, with more bravado than I felt. "His shenanigans! You guys love him, too!"

There was some nodding among the kids—they did indeed love *Farmer Duck*—and for a glorious minute I thought we had gotten away with it. But I had forgotten what an idiot Marie was.

"Yeah," she said. "That's the better book about a farmer."

Too quick, before I could say a word, Tyler snapped, "It is *not*. I want *Old MacDonald Had a Farm*!"

Honestly, if at that moment, Marie had simply begun to read *Farmer Duck* aloud, we still could have pulled it off.

We wouldn't have been unscathed, and Marie definitely deserved an opportunity to reflect on and apologize for the poor choices she had made, but we would've been home free. Instead, foolishly, she tried to reason with a three-year-old.

"Both books are about farmers, though," she said.

"Farmer Duck is a duck first," Tyler said. "He's more duck than farmer."

He was… not wrong. Marie looked to me, already out-argued by someone wearing Pull-Ups. I was going to have to step in again, I realized.

"Well, I don't know where *Old MacDonald Had a Farm* is," I said, shrugging. "So we'll just have to—"

"Let's look around for it," Bea, one of the droolers, said, cutting me and all hope of salvation off.

Dammit, Bea!

All we could do now was hope that they wouldn't spot the book hovering two feet above their heads. The kids started to wander around, searching for it. Jenny headed right for the Duplo box. Emma looked for the book under her napping mat. Tyler seemed to have a search team methodically working under his direction, like the cast of a CBS procedural. Marie and I kept in tight eye contact, making sure neither of us glanced at the shelf where we both knew she had stashed *Old MacDonald Had a Farm*.

Finally, the tension got to be too much, and I turned my back to the class to subtly glance up. To my horror, I noticed that the corner of the book was sticking out, a distinctive red triangle of the cover visible from below. Any tiny child, standing under the shelf, looking directly up, could spot the hoof of the sheep/pig.

My God, Marie. She literally had had one job. And blown it. In my peripheral vision, I saw her hand fly to her mouth as she took in what I saw, but she managed to not say anything.

Casually, so casually, I walked around the room, away from the book at first, and then leisurely, calmly, back over to it. Humming "The Wheels on the Bus" to myself, I scanned the classroom. Every child seemed to be busy searching, so I used my shoulder to bump the book back onto the shelf, fully hiding it. From the floor, Marie let out a sigh of relief.

"Hey, class, I don't think we're going to find *Old MacDonald* before it's Snack Time," I said, trying to hide my triumph. "But you guys love *Farmer Duck*."

Most of the kids obediently made their way back to the Storytime rug. A few looked sad. A few looked confused. Jenny clearly had at least three Duplo blocks crammed into her mouth. I went over to help her.

Marie opened *Farmer Duck* and took a big breath, but just then, Tyler appeared behind her. His index finger pointed upward. In the voice of an Old Testament prophet, he intoned, "It is there! On the shelf!"

If he had said it with just a bit less assurance, or if his tiny finger hadn't been pointing directly at the shelf that did, indeed, hold *Old MacDonald Had a Farm*, or if Jenny, her voice freed again, hadn't said, "Oh, wow," with quite such awe, we might've reasoned with him. Marie, newly strengthened with resolve, tried to start reading again.

But looking at his tiny, completely self-assured face, I couldn't go along with it. Tyler was absolutely correct. It was there. On the shelf. He really wanted to read that book. I caved.

SIGNS YOU MAY BE A CHARACTER IN A POPULAR CHILDREN'S BOOK

You are a bear.

If you wear clothing, your outfit is missing some key element, such as pants.

You have severe impulse-control issues, although you generally mean well.

If you are British, you have extremely small, achievable dreams, like going to the sea or having a tasty snack.

You would like a hug.

You probably do not work—surprisingly, this doesn't seem to be connected to the pantlessness—but if you do have an occupation, you are either a teacher, a maid, or the driver of a large and complicated vehicle.

You spend more time with your best friend than any actual human adult has. Ever.

That best friend takes up 80 percent less physical space than you.

Hobbies? Binge eating, hard consonants, train conducting, and the songs of the American West.

Either you are a mouse or you have surprisingly few issues with the many mice in your life.

You told the Realtor, "We're really in the market for a split-level tree."

You were created by a celebrity's book editor based on the celebrity's vague musings about her youth, you will briefly appear on the *Today* show, and then you will never be heard from again.

You either speak for the trees, or you are an increasingly abused tree who probably needs someone to speak up for it.

You'd like to say more than "Move on back" or the alphabet, but so far, no opportunity has presented itself.

If you were born before 1970, there's a very strong chance that someone reading about you will get to a certain sentence or

picture and say, "Oh, dear, that hasn't aged well," and close
your book. Forever.

Either you do not poop, or only wish to discuss poop.

Wait, is that a bowl of mush in your room?

TO MAKE US CRY

My second-grade teacher, Miss Kastler (aka Miss K), used to read aloud to my class. During my early-elementary years, our school encouraged us to read to ourselves, which was my preference, anyway. But Miss K stubbornly insisted that we were still little kids and thus, should be read *to*. She was such a good reader that I remember those times very fondly, looking forward to ending our school day by listening to a little bit more of whatever chapter book she had chosen. We made our way through lighter works—*Encyclopedia Browns*, *The Mouse and the Motorcycle*, and so on.

Toward the end of the year, our read-aloud time took an abrupt turn. Well, that might be too dramatic; it's not as if we started Allen Ginsberg's *Howl*. But Miss K did begin Wilson Rawls's 1961 classic *Where the Red Fern Grows*. It's about (and told in the adult voice of) Billy, a boy in the Ozarks who buys two hunting dogs. You probably just clutched at your heart, knowing books with dogs = sad endings. Yep, you're correct.

Where the Red Fern Grows is an adventure, a love story, and a tearjerker, all in one, in the grand tradition of *Old Yeller* and *Marley and Me*. My classmates and I were too young to know what was coming.

I should pause the story here and mention that I am a crier. I cry at expected times, when other, normal, people cry, at funerals and weddings and when athletes win Olympic medals after overcoming tremendous odds. But I also cry whenever someone else cries, a Pavlovian response.[21] There's more: I cry at mawkish television commercials, awards-show speeches, Bruce Springsteen songs (even the rousing ones like "Glory Days"), and standing ovations. Pretty trees. Small children. Poems, including those about the glories of war which I absolutely do not agree with in any way. "God Bless America" at baseball games. I cry at the same movies every time I watch them, but a little bit earlier each time, which means that when I view a film like *Field of Dreams*, I pretty much start weeping when the opening credits roll and don't stop until the ending ones begin. I think, therefore I cry, in other words. Growing up in the macho-aspirant 1980s, I was often derided by my classmates for being a crybaby, which—fair point—I was.

Back to the story. What I most remember about Miss K's reading of *Where the Red Fern Grows* is when, after many weeks of buildup, she finally got to the climax of the novel. I very much expected everything to work out just fine, despite gobs of foreshadowing dripping off the plot. I also misunderstood Miss K's warning that the rest of the book was going to be tough, as she put it, incorrectly believing she meant the

---

21 My father was a crier, too, and we ended up inadvertently egging each
    other on, frequently.

WHY WE READ   99

vocabulary was going to get harder. Oblivious, I settled down
happily at the end of a school day to listen. Almost immediately, Miss K read us the section in which a mountain lion
attacks our protagonist, Billy.[22] The dogs, Old Dan and Little
Ann, defend him and kill the lion, but not before it mortally
wounds Old Dan, who dies. I remember my jaw dropping,
shocked: a character can die in a book for kids? I had no idea!

After my shock wore off, of course I started to cry. But this
time, I was not alone. Miss K was also visibly weeping. That
a grown-up was crying (and not my dad) seemed a much bigger deal. Miss K just kept on reading, a Kleenex from the box
on her desk crumpled in her left hand. Tearing my eyes away
from my bawling teacher, I realized that my classmates were
crying, too, even some of the boys! We instinctively tried to
be quiet so that we could continue to listen closely. To my
right, Farrah threw her shoulders back and gazed at the ceil-
ing, silently sobbing, bereft. To my left, Jason covered his face
with his hands and let the sobs (quietly) rip.

Miss K continued on, through her tears. Things got worse.
Little Ann dies of grief a few paragraphs later, and then Billy
grows up and moves away and never goes back to see the red
fern growing between their graves again. This struck me as
the worst possible ending, the red fern left unseen forever.
I cried, hard. I have to be honest with you: retrospectively,
I don't quite see why that's the particularly sad part. It's just
a plant. But at the time! It was agonizing. As she closed the
book, Miss K daubed at her face. My classmates were wail-
ing. I remember putting my tiny head down on my desk, so

---

22   Imagine not knowing where this was going. But I did not!

as to let my tears just roll right off my face and onto it. We were all just so sad!

I'm trying to imagine what would have happened at any of the schools where I've worked if the principal walked down the hallway, peered into a second-grade classroom, and saw the entire class, including the teacher, openly weeping. I doubt it would go over well. I'm not sure it did go over well back then; we all went home in a sort of shell-shocked fugue state. I vaguely recollect a subsequent speech from Miss K apologizing for being overwrought.

Still, I think it's a beautiful, if somewhat deranged, memory. Sharing that communal experience, grieving together over the loss of Old Dan and Little Ann, led by a woman brave enough to let herself be so vulnerable in front of her students really made it clear to me that, like the popular song from *Free to Be... You and Me*, it was okay to cry. To be fair, I personally didn't need to learn that. If anything, I probably needed to learn that It's Okay to Stoically Hold It Together Every Once in a While. But I'm so moved now to know that we were so affected by—of all things!—a book.

Books are sly and can crack us open. They make us bring ourselves to the story. My Old Dan and Little Ann looked a lot like my own dog, Black Jack, I'm pretty sure, even though he was a different breed and never hunted for more than the fun-size chocolate bars I mistakenly left in my coat pockets. I bet my classmates each pictured different Old Dans and Little Anns, too, bearing resemblances to dogs they knew and loved, making their deaths that much more obliterating. How dare books tap into our souls like that!

In subsequent years, I would read aloud to my students from

time to time, particularly enjoying sharing some of David Sedaris's *Holidays on Ice* with my high schoolers before winter
break, a work of quite a different tone than *Where the Red Fern
Grows*. Some loved it; some fell asleep, which I never really
saw as a commentary on my performance, as high schoolers will fall asleep anywhere.[23] But I've never had anything
close to the emotional impact Miss K had on us, because I
didn't choose a sad book. That's really the key to the communal experience.

The collective catharsis a sad book can bring doesn't require that it be read aloud. The mania has faded now, but at
the end of my time teaching high school, many of my students were besotted with John Green's YA novel *The Fault in
Our Stars*, which came out in early 2012. That book… Well,
let me just say tears will be jerked. It's a very good, very sad
book about kids with cancer. Copies of *The Fault in Our Stars*
were passed around among the readers of my little school,
and because the book is unputdownable, for a few weeks, I
would frequently spot someone reading it in class, ineffec-
tively hiding it in their laps, giant tears dropping onto their
desks. I have a soft spot for kids who'd rather read than pay
attention to grammar lessons, so I usually just dropped off a
tissue as I walked by.

They might not have been reading it aloud or all at once,
but the readers were experiencing that novel together. They
talked about it in the cafeteria, on the walk home, and even
in papers and projects for my class. I eventually came to understand that while my students loved the book for many rea-

---

23   I once saw television footage of President Obama visiting a high school,
     and a student was asleep in the back of the room where he was speaking.
     'Tis their nature.

sons, at least one of them was that its tragedy allowed them to rehearse loss. How badly can something hurt? How hard can losing someone be? How awful will profound grief feel? Those answers are not always present in a sad book, but glimmers of what's ahead might be. I think I glimpsed them in Miss K's class, too.

And, of course, sad books offer us the chance to bounce back from our grief far more quickly than we can (or will or should) in real life. I'm certain that as sad as I was over Old Dan and Little Ann, I recovered by the time I got home or at least by the next morning. I recall no student of mine woebegone for more than a few minutes upon finishing *The Fault in Our Stars*, even if the story stuck with them for a long time, like *Red Fern* has for me. At the end, together, we've walked in another person's shoes (and cried in their hankies) and are better off for it—but we return to our own daily existence, somehow a little lighter, a fun-size chocolate bar in our pocket, a life to still be lived.

BECAUSE I WANTED
FREE PIZZA

I dislike our American tendency to blame our beleaguered educational system for our bad reading habits. So I'm glad I can truthfully place the blame for my tendency to read far too fast on my once-favorite dining establishment: Pizza Hut. While I would still gladly go for an extra-cheese personal pan right this minute if you're buying, it's indisputably true that Pizza Hut created the BOOK IT![24] program, and the BOOK IT! program is what messed this reader up—bad.

That's not to imply that the BOOK IT! initiative hasn't done a lot of good. According to *Mental Floss*, more than fourteen million schoolchildren have participated in the program since its inception in 1984. The idea is simple: the more books students report having read, the more prizes they earn, such as stickers, buttons, and certificates, eventually culminating in coupons for free personal pizzas.

It's infallible logic. Kids should read more. Kids like pizza.

---

24   The aggressive all-caps are their choice, not mine.

If kids read more, we'll give them free pizza. You can see why Pizza Hut went for it. I mean, free pizza is still the method we use at my university to coax our students to come to events. We also often give them free T-shirts. So does Pizza Hut's BOOK IT! program.

All of this is great, particularly for children who need a little coaxing to keep reading, especially those in families that don't get to eat out that often, so let me say quite clearly: I have no beef with the Pizza Hut BOOK IT! program. Good work, all around!

However. I was not one of the children who needed to be coaxed. I read, a lot, already: in the bathroom, in the car, in the dentist's chair, waiting for my dad to pick me and my cello up, at my brother's soccer games, and while theoretically helping my mom with dinner. I read as we drove through the raw natural beauty of Yosemite National Park and missed seeing several bears. I read during my math classes at school, when I definitely should have been listening.[25] In other words, I did not need to be enticed to read more.

I also did not need to eat more Pizza Hut pizza. This is not a commentary on my health, or on whether anyone should be eating Pizza Hut all that often, but a statement of fact. When I was a child, there was a Pizza Hut a short walk from our house, and it was my absolute favorite place to dine, which led to a weekly scene in our living room. My father wondered aloud to my mother where we should get dinner, and I would race in from three rooms away to suggest Pizza Hut. I didn't get my way all the time, but it was often enough.

I'm honestly not sure if I'm trying to tell you that the

25 I still cannot do the most basic math, including calculating a 20-percent tip.

BOOK IT! system was rigged against me, or that I was rigged against it, but anyway, I was deeply motivated and highly adept at pushing the system to its breaking point. I went for it with my whole heart, determined to earn at least one free pizza coupon a marking period. And thus, I learned the art of reading without actually understanding what I'd read.

I'm sure you're familiar. You have to read a book for some reason, and you're not that excited about it (see "Because We Had To" earlier), but you're a good person, you're not going to say you read a book if you didn't. So you run your eyes over every single line. And yet, when you get to the end, much more quickly than you should've, you'd be hard-pressed to explain even the basics of the book. It has a main character, and that main character had a problem. Maybe? Things happened, and then the problem resolved. Probably.

Most of us have done this when, say, encouraged to read a book on driving safety by our insurance company in order to get a rate reduction, or when given a book self-published by a friend who writes rhyming acrostics about their cat's nine lives. We open the cover. We scan every paragraph! No page is left unturned! No one can say we did not read the book!

Except, you know, we didn't really read the book. We *saw* every page of the book.

I taught myself to "read" this way, in a mad quest to earn pizzas and not have to go to the Jolly Roger, one of my father's favorite restaurants, which specialized in Cuisine and Decor for the Aged and had the kind of chicken strips I didn't like.

No one ever called me out for not really reading, and I didn't perceive any problems with this method myself, even as it drifted into my own, less output-oriented leisure reading. While I read some books with great attention—you will soon hear about my love for *David Bowie's Serious Moonlight*—I just didn't grasp that *all* books can be read with attention. Even the insurance pamphlet, in hindsight, probably has some good tips.

No one intervened. If anything, my method was encouraged. Almost every adult I encountered thought it was great that I read so much, and I continued to get high marks on my papers and tests in English, so bully for me, it seemed.[26] In high school, as I "read" the assigned books, like *Heart of Darkness*, I continued to faithfully run my eyes over each page. It never occurred to me that slowing down might help me comprehend them, most likely because I resented having to read them at all. I was no longer earning pizzas but still somehow believed that adding to my growing stack of books marked *Read* mattered more than what I got from the experience of reading them. No wonder I have trouble recollecting much about the thousands of books I read during my teen years. Those books had main characters, with problems... and that's about all I can remember.

It wasn't until I got to graduate school at NYU that the BOOK IT! method finally petered out for me, and thank goodness. One required class, Dramatic Criticism, was heavy on theory, heavy on reading, heavy on reading about theory. But hey, everyone knew I was a reader, that was my thing. No problem.

---

26 I want to take pains here to emphasize that my overworked English teachers are in no way to blame for my ability to bamboozle them (and pretty much everyone else, including myself) into believing I was a terrific reader.

Alas. I was miserably lost on the tests for that class. We were given lengthy quotes and asked to locate them from our (hundreds of pages) of reading and then to explain them. I could barely do this. It's apparent to me now (and you, I'm sure) why this was: I hadn't actually read the books these quotes were taken from. I had looked at them, every page. But I had, at best, skimmed them, as if the end result was going to be a pizza coupon, not a test.

I passed the class (and, God help me, the also-required Dramatic Criticism II), but what I really learned was that I was not nearly the reader I had thought I was. What followed wasn't exactly a long, dark night of the soul but more of a thoughtful amble of the midafternoon. If reading was my thing, I thought, as I wandered through Washington Square Park, another B– test in hand, and if I wasn't a particularly good reader… Well. Huh. I thought about the thousands of books I had read and couldn't remember much about. Was that who I wanted to be? How many personal-pan pizzas can one person eat, anyway?

I realized that I had to slow down, to read less in order to understand more. It wasn't easy to learn to do this. The best technique I came up with was to ask myself as I came to the end of each page if I remembered what I had just read. Not every detail, of course, but perhaps what century the book was set in? If the main characters were aliens or not? That helped.

Also, I started reading most books the way I read my coursework—with a pencil in hand, making notes if I could. I began to keep journals of my reading, and, when they became available, tracked it on apps, not (only) to keep a log of how much I read, but of what I read, of what I'm putting into my brain. This wasn't easy, and I still struggle with it. I'm a good reader, y'all, but I am an *excellent* skimmer.

Luckily for me, my subsequent career as a professor encouraged me to slow down even more. High-school students hope you miss some of their typos and nearing-deadline gibberish as you read their words, but college creative writing students do *not* like it if your critique of their story fails to grasp its basic premise because you skimmed it. They want your complete attention on their work, and they will absolutely tell you if they feel they haven't received it. Besides, they will write better, hugely better, if they feel someone is paying attention, so I was, and am, very motivated to read closely.

Some of those very same creative writing students have mentioned the Pizza Hut BOOK IT! program from their own childhoods, and I'm pleased to report that their stories vary. Some, like me, still can't believe they got rewarded for running a long con. Others didn't like Pizza Hut. And some did read more because they wanted the stickers, the buttons, the T-shirt, and the pizza. So, well done, Pizza Hut! What began with you pushing your product has led some of your recipients to pursue degrees in English and a lifetime of reading.

Sometimes I miss my skim-like-the-wind days. I would give anything to be back at the Jolly Roger with my dad, bored and sneaking peeks at the book in my lap. I know that the next time I tour through Yosemite, I'll be the one driving, so no reading will occur.[27] And I would really, truly love if someone would give me a free pizza for reading. Or a cookie.

---

27   Nor should it! Look around. It's Yosemite!

A glass of water? Or a Netflix deal to adapt this book into a long-running series? Thanks.

And yet, for all my nostalgia, I like the way I read now. There are stacks of books in my house that will never be depleted, not just because I'm constantly adding to them—true—but because I simply can't get to them all, not in this lifetime, not at the slower, more attentive pace at which I now read. Reading is no longer a race that I might win, but a lifelong companion, a dear friend who's always there for me but never, ever asks for a slice.

TO FIND THE MAIN POINT

At my very first job teaching secondary-school English at Stella Maris, my first-year students were assigned *The Diary of a Young Girl* (often called *Anne Frank's Diary*) as summer reading. This was not my idea but that of the teacher I was hired to sub for, a job that originally was to run about six weeks but ended up lasting four years. The original teacher also left a test on *Diary* to give to her class in the first week of school. These days, I almost never give tests at all, and I certainly would *never* hand out a test written by anyone else, but back then, not only was I obliged to follow the original teacher's lesson plan, I was quite glad to use her test, because I had no idea how to write one.

This is all preamble/apology to explain to you why I gave my new students a test that asked them, vis-à-vis *The Diary*, "What is the main point of this book?"

Ugh.

This is a bad question. Books don't have main points, or

at least this kind of book doesn't. I suppose that a book titled *Let's Learn How to Draw Penguins with Common Household Implements* has a point, or, more precisely, a purpose. But Anne Frank didn't write the book for public consumption, and even as its only audience/reader, she must have had several purposes: to entertain herself, to remember what was happening around her and to her, to analyze her motivations and those of her family, to provide succor in a time of need… in short, all of the reasons why those who keep diaries do so. You could argue that her publisher (or her father, who located a publisher) had a point to make, but even there, I'd say that there was more than one—memorial, reminder, warning—not easily reduced to a singular main point, written on a blank line about three inches long.

The woman I was subbing for was a great teacher, so I feel very sure that she phrased her question that way because that's the sort of language standardized tests use. We English teachers of Stella Maris were, I would learn, always aware of the looming English Regents, a must-pass standardized test that asks questions very similar to this one. Passing at least five Regents is required to matriculate from most New York City high schools, private and public. Teachers are shamed for *teaching to the test*, but if we didn't, many of our students wouldn't graduate.

I've always hated this particular kind of test question. Identifying the main point in a reading passage is a skill, I suppose, but one I've had to call upon exceedingly rarely, and never outside of academia (and I make my living reading stuff!). Yet this way of thinking about literature, of distilling it, really, burning away all its character and wit and context and mood to a short phrase that very often insinuates that the author wrote with some lesson or moral to impart, is so often on tests that students have come to understand finding the main idea as the proper way to think about literature. I should know, as I've certainly spent a goodly portion of my college-teaching days trying to yank readers toward something more profound and less reductive. There are other, much more vital skills that can be learned through reading, even for those who have no intention of writing a word more than they have to: empathy, the play of language on the ear, the way words can change one's thinking, the gifts of imagination to our weary minds. But these are not measurable by standardized tests, so we ask our students to find, again and again, the main point. We couch the question in different forms, but it's the same, every time.

I didn't know that yet, but I felt it. As I glanced over the test before handing it out, I paused at that question, my Spidey sense piqued. But it was not my test to change, so I handed it out to my classroom of first-years, and the room got quiet.

When it came time to grade the tests, I was—no surprise—skeptical. The supposedly correct answer to the question from the answer key I was given is lost to the winds of time, but it was something along the lines of *Bad things happen, but people are still good*, which… yes, sure, that is a main point of *The Diary of a Young Girl*, but also of the film *The Hangover*. Given that it was a summer-reading assignment, which meant that the students had received not a whit of context or additional help, I decided to accept pretty much anything that at least gestured toward an understanding of the themes of the book. Many of the girls wrote something about the

Holocaust being bad, or about Anne's moving optimism in the face of encompassing evil. Sure, the Holocaust was definitely bad. Full points.

However, a select few wrote something along the lines of *Anne got to kiss a boy before she died*. Now, myself, I would struggle to articulate the main point of *The Diary of a Young Girl* in a sentence. But while I may not have known exactly how to word the/a main point, I *definitely* knew it was not that Anne got to kiss a boy. If the question had been *What do you remember about this book?* or *What part of the book was most interesting to you?* or *When you asked your friend to quickly summarize a book you had not read as the teacher passed out this test, what did she say?* this would have been an acceptable answer. Or I'd have allowed an attempt to broaden the question, an argument that the better thing to ask was what we readers find particularly devastating, to which *A young woman has a brief spark of romance before her flame is forever cut down* would be a great answer. But just *She got to make out?* No.

These days, I'd declare the question to have been poorly worded (my bad, not theirs), tell the class that, and award everyone credit. But I hadn't learned that was an option yet. I marked the snogging answers wrong; there was no right answer, but, somehow, there was a wrong answer.

Not a single student argued with me about their grade. It was early in the year, and they didn't know me, of course, but I had expected some haggling. But, as is too often the case in an American high-school English class, students took a flawed test, which they sensed to be an attempt to measure unmeasurable qualities, got a few wrong, and decided that the flaw was with them, not the assignment. Or the teacher. Or those endless standardized tests. They decided, in short, that they were bad readers who couldn't understand books. That they were too shallow to correctly identify the Main Point.

And here, dear readers, I hope you begin to sense one of the reasons why my students no longer liked reading as much at fourteen as they did when they were three. I would see this consistently throughout the next four years at Stella Maris: students who were perfectly good readers, and who might have enjoyed a lot of the assigned literature, did not like reading well-written books because of how their reading was evaluated. They read with the test hanging over their heads. Imagine watching a favorite television show, knowing that at the end, someone will be asking you what the main theme of the episode was[28]—it's going to at least dampen the fun.

And those were the students who bothered to do the reading. One of the other English teachers filled innocent-newbie-teacher me in on the truth that many didn't complete the summer reading at all, guessing correctly that a friend's quick summary adequately prepared them to get a B on the test, and while a B wasn't great, it was good enough. It was hard to blame the girls, really, since they knew nothing else would be asked of them regarding the assigned reading, and thus its use to them ended once they turned in the test.

Well. I found the entire thing very disheartening. Not only did the entire meshuga seem disrespectful to Anne Frank's memory, it seemed to disrespect reading in general. I still loved to read, and annoyingly I felt everyone else should, too. Even at the advanced age of thirty, I was plowing through

---

28   "Chandler learned that he should have just told Janice the truth. Honesty is the best policy." Oh, I want to die just from writing this as a joke.

books at the rate of several a week. My commute to Stella Maris was ninety minutes each way, and I had to pass the time; reading made it almost a pleasure. I wanted my students to have that joy, too.

Yet on my own bus ride home on the day I gave back the girls' tests, I actually didn't read much. After watching them care *only* about the grades I had written at the top, I stared out the window, watching the Marine Parkway Bridge roll by. By then, I understood that not everyone, perhaps not most people, felt about reading the way I did, but I couldn't believe how many of them hadn't really read the book at all. They didn't see anything wrong with having skimmed a summary online, either. It was a moral neutral for them.

When I was a high schooler, I remembered, the prospect of a class discussion had motivated me to read when I was less than excited about the book. I wanted to share my thoughts but also hear what others got out of the reading, too. That made literature come alive for me, and I genuinely understood it better after the discussions. It helped me warm to the challenge of more difficult books, knowing I was on the journey together with my classmates.

So, smugly sure that I had found *the* key to unlocking my students' interest in reading, I initiated a discussion about *Diary* in class the next day. This, I felt sure, was going to get at the real complexity of the book, to help them realize what this primary source has to teach us about humanity and the way we treat each other. I wanted to first discuss what we found memorable or haunting about the book, yes, but also why they thought it has such staying power.

My students had a quick answer for the second question—

"Because teachers like you keep assigning it, Ms. Reed"—and interpreted the first question as, you guessed it, "What is the main point of this book?" Resignedly, they parroted back to me whatever they had written on their tests, except for the girls who thought the point was that Anne got to kiss a boy before she died. They just stared at their desks. It wasn't long before everyone was staring—at their desks, out the window, at their hands, at each other. Anything to avoid looking at me and my surprise insistence that we were going to spend more than one class period on the only classic book I know of written by a girl their age.

Well, this is another disaster, I thought to myself. I was about to give up and move us on to something else when, into the silence, one of the girls in the back said, "I think she wrote it to show us how to be brave."

It took me a minute, but I nodded my thanks to her and reminded the class that while Anne Frank had not written for us, I surely agreed that part of her book's appeal remains the bravery the Franks, and those who lived with them, and those who hid them, showed in the face of evil. There was some nodding around the classroom; they were starting to buy into the conversation. Students at that age are thinking about what kind of adults they might be, and the idea of choosing to be a brave person sounded interesting.

I asked the class something along the lines of "Do you think you would have been as brave?" and asked them to write down their answers.

Alas, this was a poorly worded question: I didn't know that you should never, ever give students a yes/no question to discuss or write about, if you can avoid it. Such a setup asks them to choose one of two roads. In this case, one is a paved high-way that leads to approval and praise, and the other is a rambling, potholed dead end of admitting that you're human. *Of course* they're going to say that they would have been as brave!

So, yeah, most of them said they would have protected the Franks. Already aware of the failure of my gambit,[29] I pushed back a bit, pointing out that while there were indeed *many* people who bravely hid their fellow citizens from the Nazis, millions of Jewish people were slaughtered in concentration camps, so it was mathematically impossible that *most* people were brave. Right, the girls said, most people are bad, but not us, we're good.

"We've read *The Diary of a Young Girl*," one student pointed out. "So we know what's what."

"Yes," I said, "but millions of people have read *The Diary of a Young Girl*."

"And there hasn't been another Holocaust!"

"Whoa!" said one student. "My home—*Rwanda*. Hello!"

The discussion was turning into an argument, one that I wasn't comfortable facilitating on my ninth day of teaching secondary English. Was it time to send them to lunch yet, maybe, please? Then, miracle of miracles, one girl asked to read her answer. I allowed it with the eagerness of a drowning woman grabbing a life preserver. I'm paraphrasing, but the essence of what she had written was this.

I would not have protected the Franks. I know we are supposed to say that we would have, and I would have known that and felt like I should, but I wouldn't have actually done it because I like being alive,

---

29   I should have titled my memoir about teaching *Already Aware of the Failure of My Gambit*.

and I would have been scared of the Nazis. I would've felt real bad about it, but I wouldn't have hid them. Maybe I would have tried to help them some other way, but not like that.

Her words lingered in the room for a few moments, rich and heavy and sad. Talk about bravery. That would turn out to be one of the bravest things I've ever seen a student do: willingly admit her lack of moral courage.

And then other girls started to agree—they wouldn't have been as brave, either.

"She almost got herself killed," one girl said with horror about Miep Gies, who had helped hide the Franks.

"The Nazis would just kill you right there," another said. "I'm afraid of guns. I'd die if someone just pointed one at me."

"You'd have to live with that guilt for the rest of your life," said another. "But you'd have the rest of your life to try to make up for it."

The girl from Rwanda said quietly, "My family didn't help anyone."

"Well," I remember thinking, as I shuffled to the side of the classroom and listened as they talked to each other, "we found the main point."

Here's what I learned that day. Books do have a main point after all, but it changes for each reader, and for each group of people puzzling their way to it. There are so many different things to learn from *Diary*, but what our group had settled on was a stark reminder that knowing the right thing to do is not necessarily the first step toward doing it. Every one of us grasped that protecting innocent fellow humans was the only morally correct choice. Yet only one of us was willing to admit what had to be true: that if this has been asked of most of us, we wouldn't have done it.

In my recollection the discussion gradually drifted into wondering just how hot Peter had been. Yet I am sure that the book had more of an impact on those girls because of the conversation. They'd take more tests about books, some from me, because we had to give them grades, and because their parents were paying us to make sure they'd ace, or at least pass, several difficult standardized tests on their way to college. But I never again conflated the understanding displayed on a test with what a student had to say or write in a discussion or a paper. I began to prefer inching toward deeper under-standings, with the knowledge that the destination may not be reached, rather than asking for pat answers that required no real reading and no real thought.

I often return to the memory of that classroom discussion when faced with lesson planning, specifically for a class that I know should be a discussion. The truth is that discussions can be a total pain in the ass to implement, even with moti-vated, engaged students. Discussions are wearying for the fa-cilitator—simultaneously listening and trying to make sure everyone gets heard, encouraging the reluctant, taming the demanding—all the while attempting to make sure we don't wander so far afield that our discussion of *The Liars' Club* has somehow become about last night's *Riverdale*.[30]

But still, in my class, we discuss because standardized tests aren't where an assigned book comes alive for those who haven't been won over by the reading of it; that happens in

---

30   It's happened. I'll own it.

discussion, in the thinking. To be honest, when teaching a book for the fourth or fifth or twentieth time, discussions are what I look forward to—that's when I'm going to see how the unique people in my classroom are going to interpret stories I already know so well. They always surprise me, revealing ideas brand-new but valid. They are the main point.

BECAUSE FAILURE IS MOST DEFINITELY AN OPTION

Like many bright, anxious teenagers as well as most astronauts, I used to believe that failure was not an option. This was particularly true about books and reading, because even in my youth, I already sort of thought of myself as writer, and I believed that in order to demonstrate what an excellent writer I was, I automatically should be very good at all book-adjacent things. To make a mistake about literature meant that I was not going to be a writer. What a punishingly high bar I set for myself.

Thus, more than once, I did not admit I was unfamiliar with a famous work of literature when it came up in conversation, feeling that I, a writer—sort of—should know it already. For quite a long time, this worked out well enough. I even bluffed my way through a conversation about *The Bacchae* at a college interview and got in. Of course, I now teach at a college, so I realize that most admissions officers expect prospective students to bluff their way through at least 30 percent of the interview, so this wasn't the triumph I thought it was at the time.

Anyway, the terrible habit ended one evening at a close friend's high-school graduation party, when his father said something to me about the celebration looking *Gatsby-esque*. No problem. Although I hadn't read it, I was sure I knew what *The Great Gatsby* was about.

"Yeah," I said to my friend's dad. "All we need are some flappers!"

He laughed. "And some bathtub gin!"

"Yeah!" I said, warming to it. "And elephants! And some clowns! And maybe a lion tamer!"

His smile faded into confusion because, dear reader, it turns out that *The Great Gatsby* is not about a circus magician in the 1920s as I thought.

Would it have killed me to just admit that I—an eighteen-year-old in Johnstown, Pennsylvania—had not quite gotten around to reading F. Scott Fitzgerald's classic? No, of course not. I should've. My friend's dad would hardly have cared. But I was afraid of seeming uncultured, uncouth, dumb, all of which I was, at least a little.

I had skin in the game, though, which always makes such mistakes hurt more. I was trying hard to be somewhat culturally sophisticated. I watched *Monty Python* and read Thornton Wilder. I owned more than one book by Thomas Merton.[31] I had seen *Gigi*, so I knew what a courtesan was (kinda). I started subscribing to the *New Yorker* when I was fourteen, driven, again, by some primordial sense that I was a writer, and writers and the *New Yorker* were bound up together. I

---

31   I still do, and I still have not read them.

WHY WE READ 125

understood about 40 percent of what I read in the magazine, almost all of that in the restaurant and movie reviews, but I sure looked smart (I thought) carrying around the latest issue.

I'm hardly alone in trying to vamp my way through literary knowledge. My colleague, the novelist Irina Reyn, tells a great story about how someone mispronounced the title *The Namesake* (making it sort of rhyme with *namaste*) when introducing the author, Jhumpa Lahiri, in front of hundreds of people. When I was a library page, a patron returned *The Catcher in the Rye* in a huff, saying that there wasn't enough baseball for his taste.[32] A friend of mine thought that the *whale*'s name was Ishmael. Another friend was fifty pages into a Meg Wolitzer novel before she realized that every other page was stuck together ("I kept saying to my husband how proud I was to be reading something so experimental!" she told me). Entire tenth-grade classrooms have concluded that *The Crucible* is about actual witches. The list of stupid things smart people have said and thought in the general category of Books is endless.

Each of the above mistakes is fixable, although learning how to pronounce *Namesake* is probably simpler than redirecting a class intent on hocus-pocusing Arthur Miller's work. I could have read *The Great Gatsby* after being gently corrected by my friend's dad. I suspect that even just taking a closer look at its classic cover would have been enough to gently nudge me away from whatever a circus magician is.[33] Alas, embarrassed, I instead took the entirely human, if re-

---

32 That's fair.

33 I think the giant glasses misled me? Don't circus magicians, whatever they are, wear giant glasses?

grettable, stance of refusing to read *The Great Gatsby* for many subsequent years.

Somehow, in my mind, my initial misunderstanding imbued the book with a level of sophistication and craft that I could never comprehend. I was deeply afraid that I just would not, you know, *get* the book, so I avoided it at every possible opportunity. I don't want to oversell this, it's not as if Jay Gatsby was waiting for me around every corner, but as a high-school English teacher, it wasn't completely remote from my existence. Some dodging was involved. If you have read *The Great Gatsby*, you must be shaking your head ruefully at younger me, for the book is both quite short and highly readable. I mean, it's about tragic rich people, for heaven's sake. Who doesn't have time for some tragic rich people and their absolutely ghastly parties?

While my history with *Gatsby* was particularly fraught, I think this fear of a book, or some books, or all books is everywhere, pervasive in our culture. I have a lot of very smart, highly educated friends who love reading, and yet I find that universally, they also feel intimidated by it, too. All have considered reading a particular book, enticed by a cover, a review, a friend's recommendation, but put it back on the shelf at the library or bookstore because they just didn't think they would *get* it.

When I assigned Elena Ferrante's beautiful, troubling novel *My Brilliant Friend* to a reading group of older adults I was leading, more than half told me that they were so happy I chose it because "I wanted to read it but never would have picked it up on my own." Why not? It looked "too hard" or "was more of a *New York Times* book than what I usually read," or the fact that it was translated from Italian to English was too unnerving.[34] There's no doubt that all of us got more out of the book because of our thoughtful discussions, but I feel sure that group of intelligent folks who—this is key— *wanted* to understand the book could have gotten pretty far toward their goal on their own, had they tried. When we parted, I exhorted them to keep reading Ferrante's work, and I hope that they did. But I suspect some didn't try, even if they wanted to.

Fear curdles and ruins when we let it drive our reading choices. We build up an expectation for a book before reading it, and then, when it turns out to be something different than what we anticipated, we take it as proof that we don't know what we're doing, and our reading is wrecked. We swear off short stories because we misunderstood one of them, once, back in the late '90s.[35] We decide that only people who got to take Intro to Comp should read so-called important books. We try a different genre of novel and can't follow the plot, so we rush back to our familiar type or, worse, just stop reading. Someone makes us feel badly for having not read *Their Eyes Were Watching God*, so instead of just reading that book (or shrugging and saying we'll get around to it[36]), we decide not to talk about books with anyone, ever again. We reread a book we once loved and now see it's full of plot holes and

---

34 Translations particularly freak people out, and I include myself in that group. Hilarious, because the entire point was to make the book more accessible.

35 Yes, this was me, for a while, too.

36 I didn't get around to it until I was assigned it while working on my MFA (thanks, Gayle!), and darn if it isn't great.

repetitious adverbs, so we decide we were stupid for liking it, and that we have no taste and should stop reading, instead of recognizing that books speak to us differently at different ages. Too many people remember how helpless they felt while trying to interpret the passages on those god-awful standardized tests and how those tests shook their confidence and turned them off from reading entirely.

Fear of looking dumb, of feeling dumb, of being dumb. Every time we crack open a cover and turn to the first page, we are taking a risk that we are not going to *get* it, a hefty blow to our sense of self. Because we live in a culture that sees failure as bad, instead of something that happens to literally everyone all the time, we back away once we fail, or even before. But that means that we keep backing ourselves into a smaller and smaller corners, with fewer of those wonderful books available to us, and thus, fewer opportunities to be entertained, to be educated, to see someone else's life.

Whew. It's a lot, I know. I think about this all the time because of my work. In my creative writing classes, there are often upper-level students who've completed most or all of their necessary coursework for some impressive major or other (engineering! pre-med! pre-law!) and are at last taking the courses they *want* to take, like mine. They frequently pop up in my Readings in Contemporary Fiction class, full of excitement (they loved reading, back in the day, and miss it) but also fear (they've stopped reading, usually because it was ruined for them in one of the ways I've mentioned above, and now they don't know if they can go back to it). They read fiction for my class because they have to, and then they realize that 1) it is not so hard after all, and 2) they still really like it. I've seen this pattern so many times, and I'm grateful to be a part of it, but it didn't have to go that way. No one should need a good teacher to rescue reading for them. Permission does not have to be granted to read.

Here's the truth: we can read whatever we want, whenever we want.

Another truth: it's highly empowering to read the book we thought we would never *get*. This is advice I had to learn myself, by the way. I finally read *The Great Gatsby* when I learned it was a mainstay of the English curriculum at Stella Maris. *Gatsby* was such a standard that there was no getting around it: I would need to teach it to my tenth graders. That I had already read it was just assumed. That I did not have a particular psychological block about it was even more assumed.

Ever so occasionally, I can get through a fraught ordeal by simply telling myself that it's not a fraught ordeal, so long as I act quickly. I picked up a copy of *The Great Gatsby* and began reading it on my lunch break on the very day I realized I'd have to teach it. It took maybe two sentences for me to realize all that I've already said—it's easy, short, highly readable:

> *In my younger and more vulnerable years my father gave me some advice that I've been turning over in my mind ever since.* Whenever you feel like criticizing anyone, *he told me,* just remember that all the people in this world haven't had the advantages that you've had.

Not to belabor the point, but please look over those sentences again. They are easily understood. *The Great Gatsby* has depth and sophistication (Why *does* Daisy stay with Tom, and why *does* Gatsby still long for her? Those are grown-up concerns.) but not a single word in those two sentences is out of reach for someone at an eighth-grade reading level. I read the entire book within the day and started teaching it a few days later, the incident with my friend's dad now transformed into an anecdote instead of an ongoing minor trauma.

Now, I understand my anecdote here works because I was hung up on a book that's not very difficult to understand, but I think the realization—just pick up the book and start reading it—applies no matter how difficult the work actually is. Of course, don't set yourself up for instant failure. Read the book in a language you understand, for one thing. Don't start this process with Judith Butler's *Gender Trouble*. You know I'm a big advocate of context, so if you're starting Boccaccio's *The Decameron*, maybe read up on it a bit before you dive in: scroll through Wikipedia or read a copy with a good introduction. But, basically, put away your phone, get a nice drink of some kind, plop yourself into a comfy chair if you can, and just start reading. That's how books work.

You have to accept that you may need to reread. This advice at first sounds annoying, I know. I can hear you saying, "Oh, sure, Shannon, because my life is made of time, so why not waste my endless moments beginning *Don Quixote*[37] over and over?" Well, point granted, none of us have a ton of free time. But reading the opening sentences or paragraphs until you're pretty sure you understand them is going to do you a lot of good: acclimate you to the style and tone of the book, make sure you have what are usually key facts (the narra-

---

37 I chose this title because it ranks first on the Want to Read, But Scared to Read list, I've found.

tive stance, for example) all set before you get too far in, and, not for nothing, allow you to consider whether this book is actually one you want to read at all. There's nothing worse than intending to read a book for pleasure but realizing that it brings you none, unless it's reading a book that could bring you pleasure but hasn't been able to do so since you're not properly situated in it.[38]

You may also need to give it some time to engage you. I usually advocate for reading ten to fifty pages, depending on how rewarding you're finding it, no matter how slowly you have to go, before stopping, but remember that I cannot actually see you throw *Don Quixote* across the room after your fifth time through the first four paragraphs. You do you. And I hope you find that saying *I gave* Don Quixote *a good try, but it wasn't for me* is much more empowering than saying *I'm not smart enough to read* Don Quixote.

Alternatively, read all of *Don Quixote* without understanding some of it, if that brings you pleasure. My students always look at me as if I have sprouted a tail when I tell them that they can read a difficult book without understanding every single aspect of it. I sometimes assign Edward P. Jones's wonderful novel *The Known World*, which is written with an omniscient narrator who travels through the minds of dozens of characters. My students, raised on first-person, present-tense YA, have rarely encountered a book like this, and it's definitely a challenge to read, so they certainly are not going to grasp every aspect of it. *The Things They Carried* is rich and beautiful but very tied to the Vietnam War, which some of

---

38   This was my exact experience with *Wuthering Heights*.

my students have never learned a whit about. *Homegoing* is highly readable, but author Yaa Gyasi has partially set it in times and places (e.g., the 1700s and Ghana) not terribly familiar to many of my American students. But this is all fine, I reassure the students. You need not wring every drop of meaning and insight from the novel on your first read. Focus on what you find engaging: the characters, the plot, the dialogue, whatever you can grab a hold of.[39]

Whatever happens, whether you love the book, or like the book, or finish but hate the book, or just hate the book so much you drive immediately to your nearest Goodwill to dispose of it properly, you did it: you read something that challenged you. Now, try another book! Read out of your genre, read a book you didn't actually pick up in high school, read a book you saw in the *New York Times*. Whatever you find a little scary, give it a try. Failure is very much an option. It's how we grow.

---

39 I do advise rereading if they liked it, but I obviously have no power to make this happen.

BUT NOT SHAKESPEARE!

I have many hills upon which I'm willing to die, but none is so deeply held as this: plays—dramas, comedies, playscripts, what have you—are supposed to be heard. Ideally, plays are to be *enacted* or *performed*, but if that's not possible, they should at least be read aloud. It baffles me that anything less than this is accepted in our schools.

As a theatre major in college and grad school, I had to read (silently, to myself, I mean) no end of plays, everything from ancient Greek works to those so new the scripts weren't even bound yet. Over the years, like my classmates, I tried to teach myself how to leave space for the visual elements of the production that did not yet exist: the actors in a space, the sound design, the lighting, the costumes, and other technical elements that would shape the experience of the play. I didn't find this easy to do, even when provided with a set design mock-up or a soundtrack for the musical. As an actor in training, I also should have been able to imagine how a character might look or sound saying the lines I was reading, but while I did better at that than with the tech elements, I still wasn't very adept, and I didn't get cast very often, at least partly because of my lack of skill. Inevitably, when seeing the actual production, I would hear another actor deliver a line or a speech with some specific choice made—in anger, in sadness, thoughtlessly, with passion—and feel delight (and chagrin) at how they had unlocked meaning in words which I had seen as stagnant on the page. It was only when the text was brought to life that I began to really see and understand it.

Theater is often said to be a collaborative art, which is often interpreted as *a bunch of people made those choices*. Certainly true but not quite it. Instead of thinking of collaboration as an aspect of theater, I think of it as the very lifeblood of the art form, the electricity jolting through the monster. Without the people, the play is not theater. It's a sort of half-formed thing.

And yet—if you think you hear me dragging out my soapbox here, yep, please clear some space in the town square—in education we mostly hand students that half-formed thing, the script, and tell them to read it to themselves. As an addendum, we also tell them that the person who wrote the words they're reading was a genius, the greatest writer of all time. I refer here, of course, to Kid Rock. No, no, I'm kidding. It's Shakespeare.

I'm not casting stones. I've done this: overhyped Shakespeare and then wondered why my students at THSB, the theater arts–themed public high school in South Brooklyn where I worked after Stella Maris, were not completely enthralled by reading *Hamlet*.

Let me stop for a minute and say, good Lord. *Hamlet!* I
started with *Hamlet!* Not even one of the Shakespearean plays
that at least starts off with someone helpfully saying to the audience *Hello, how's your day been, let's do a show, shall we?* No,
I went with *Hamlet*, which begins with two dudes named
Francisco and Bernardo in Elsinore,[40] discussing how quiet
the night watch has been. They're then joined by two more
dudes, Horatio and Marcellus, who worry about a ghost recently spotted. Worse, the words used in their conversation
include *tush, tush, apparition, assail, illume, unfold* (not the way
we use it), and *the Dane.*

Looking up from his textbook, a student pointed to that
word and said, "Like, a Great Dane?"

I said, "Well, no. Like someone from Denmark."

"Denmark sounds like a grocery store," another student
said. "Does this play take place in a Key Foods?"

And that is about where everything ground to a halt in
my classroom on the day we began *Hamlet.* You could feel
the energy leeching out. Several kids put their heads down
on their desks and drifted off to a dreamworld where no one
said *tush, tush.* I watched another let the script slip out of her
hands, where it bounced off her desk and onto the ground.
She didn't even bother to pick it up. That's what she thought
of Shakespeare. A genius? Please.

A recurrent motif in my teaching life are long thinks on
bus and train rides across New York City, wherein I try to
figure out what I did wrong at school that day and make a
plan to teach better the next day. In this case, I fretted all the

---

40   Wherever that is; I do not know even now, at 48.

way from Canarsie to the 2 stop for the Brooklyn Museum, a twenty-minute journey, before I recollected one of my college professors thundering about how we must read Shakespeare aloud.

Oh! Duh! We needed to read the play aloud! My professor had also gone on about iambic pentameter and encoded meaning and the rhythm of the sounds in the words (all very good and valid), but most of my class was nowhere near understanding that (and I was not prepared to try to get them there). I just wanted my students to be interested in the dead king's ghost. Or to understand that there was a dead king's ghost. That the whole play wasn't just the four dudes gossiping on a wall.

I tried again in class the next day. Thankfully, it was a theatre-arts school so I didn't have any trouble rounding up a cast pretty quickly, and we set off on our Shakespearean quest again, back to Francisco and Bernardo and their fairly boring discussion of how the night was going.[41] But at least this time we kept going, and they did indeed learn that there was a ghost. And we had buy-in.

I'm not going to lie to you: *Hamlet* remains four hundred years old whether you read it to yourself or aloud. It's not as if *tush, tush* now made sense.[42] We still needed to pick our way through, making good use of the scripts which helpfully had a more modern "translation" on each page. Occasionally,

---

41   We decided that the play begins this way to give everyone a chance to quiet down in their seats before the ghost appears. A candy-unwrapping opportunity, in other words.

42   Although I will note that I heard *tush, tush* in casual conversation throughout the rest of the school year.

we read the translation on its own, but faced with language like "Should I keep being alive, or should I die? That's what I'm thinking about," my students often preferred to go back and read the original aloud: "To be, or not to be. That is the question." You don't have to completely understand poetry to be moved by it.

I ended up doing a lot of quarterbacking, running through the plot points to come.[43] I would say something like "Okay, so in this scene, we're going to meet Hamlet's mom, and she has a *lot* going on, her husband was murdered, and she turned around and married his brother, and she knows Hamlet doesn't love this," which created some signposts for whoever was reading Gertrude. We stopped and started. We skipped ahead—people forget how long *Hamlet* is and how much is often cut. We admitted—I admitted—I did not know what something meant. We did not try to understand every word, or every line, or really, even every speech. (Sorry to Laertes, but I don't think we got you, like, at all.)

At the end of the play—"Wow, everyone is completely dead," someone observed—I saw all of our extra effort was worth it. We sat back in our seats, spent and proud of ourselves: we had read Shakespeare. Sitting in a chair and reading something to yourself takes far less time and energy and also draws fewer administrators to your classroom door, wondering why there's so much noise. But here's the thing: by the end, my students understood the play. Any one of them could give you an accurate rundown of the events, the characters and the themes. They could quote it.

---

43   That's what quarterbacks do, right?

Some even liked it. One young man really loved it, seeing Hamlet's inability to act in his own confusion about post–high school life. Some students had theories about why the play had lasted. ("People like blood, yo.") Some felt Shakespeare was overrated. Some really just held on to *tush, tush.* One girl gave Ophelia's monologue as her audition for a college theatre program (and got in). Some told me that we should read *Macbeth* next. Some said we should never read a play again. One young man had taken up a personal grudge against Polonius, who "deserved what he got."

Obviously, I appreciate or agree with some of these opinions more than others, but they're all valid responses to *Hamlet*. The students had actually taken in the play, and it had moved them—to joy or sorrow, distaste or intrigue. And I'm absolutely sure that would not have happened had we just continued reading the script to ourselves. Who am I kidding? They would not have continued reading the script to themselves. Perhaps a few would have tried, but whether mentally or in actuality, they mostly would have let the script slip out of their hands, onto their desk, and onto the floor.

There are many reasons to read Shakespeare—after all, he was a genius, I'm reliably told—but what I want most for my students is for them to feel that they *can*. No writer is too difficult for them, not even one from hundreds of years ago who used funny words and did not have a phone. Why make something already challenging more difficult? Plays are meant to be spoken, a simple change from the usual way of reading that honors the form Shakespeare wrote in and makes his words more accessible.

Plays should be read aloud. Period. I have died on my hill. Now, will someone help me drag this soapbox back into storage?

SIGNS YOU MAY BE A CHARACTER IN A SHAKESPEAREAN PLAY

You are dead, but still speaking.

You are dead, not speaking, just one of a dozen other corpses scattered around.

You are not dead, but you will be presently.

You are a king, or the relation of a king, and you are going to die, if you are not already dead.

You are a fairy, although your grudges seem pretty typically human.

You alone (apparently) can see the large crowd of people gathered to watch you and your companions. You decide to tell the crowd your most private thoughts from time to time.

Most of the people in the crowd don't seem to quite follow what you're saying, except when you pop off with "Out, damn spot!" and then everyone elbows each other and nods appreciatively.

You have a habit of falling in love with close friends when they're in drag.

You, the only woman, are surrounded by eighty men.

You fervently hate your very best friend.

You, a witch suffused with mysterious and otherworldly powers, mostly want to use them to mess with this dude Macbeth, whom you've never met before.

You know quite a few twins, and those twins are always up for shenanigans.

Daddy. Issues.

Mommy Issues, too, but somehow they still relate back to Daddy. Issues.

If you're named something like "Boy," good luck to ya.

You have exited, pursued by a bear.

TO FEEL LESS ALONE

When I taught English at THSB, I had a student, Carla, who loved books. *Loved* them. Books were her *thing*. Although we had virtually nothing else in common, we shared an immense love for books, and that was enough.

One day, after school, she was complaining, correctly, that our school library was both "sad and whack," so much so that she couldn't find a classic there that she thought she ought to read.

"You should look for it at the public library, Carla. They can order it for you if—"

"Nah, I don't mess with the public library, Ms. Reed."

She made this sound like a centuries-long feud. But when I questioned her further, she just shrugged and said, "I can't afford it."

It took me a moment to grasp that Carla did not know that the public library was free. It makes sense. If you had no experience with public libraries, you, too, would be suspicious of the premise: you get to just go in? And take a bunch of books? Home? At no cost? For a couple of weeks? That *is* whack.

Getting to tell a student that their heart's desire actually exists—and that they can access it immediately—is a singular pleasure of the teaching life. I had the joy of informing Carla that getting a library card cost nothing, and that taking books out wasn't going to cost her a dime, either.

"What now," she said.

I made shooing motions with my hands. There were practically Road Runner puffs of air as she ran out of my classroom on her way to the nearest public library.

The next day, she stopped by before school to show me her finds. Touched that she'd lugged the entire stack of books in just so I could see them, I held and appreciated each in turn. It was a great selection, a lovely mix of the Japanese manga she adored, the classic she had wanted, and another paperback she grabbed because the girl on the cover was young, Black, and queer like her.

"There are more of these," she said, pointing to the last one.

I'd seen her carrying one particular book about a young, Black, queer young woman protagonist around before, almost like a talisman. But I could tell that being in the library, and seeing that there were other books about queer young Black women—not just one, but *many*—well, that had changed her somehow. It was not the same Carla standing in front of me. She felt seen, in a good way.

Instead of trying to express all of that, though, I just said, "I feel like you found your place."

"Oh, Ms. Reed," she said, "I have!" As she put her books

back in her bag, she said quietly, almost to herself, "All my best friends are at the library."

It's easy to forget how lonely adolescence feels for just about everyone. While we begin to understand who we want to be, we're simultaneously not able to become that person because of our youth, lack of experience, underdeveloped brains, surrounding community, and pitiful finances. It's kind of like what *This American Life* host Ira Glass said about the gap between having good taste and being able to produce work in good taste: "For the first couple of years you make stuff, it's just not that good. It's trying to be good, it has potential, but it's not. But your taste, the thing that got you into the game, is still killer. And your taste is why your work disappoints you." Just substitute *yourself* for the *stuff you're making*, and you'll remember how awful adolescence is. Even worse, we often lack proof that there are others like us out there, as Carla did, no matter how we define ourselves—which can be profoundly lonely. Scariest of all, we might begin to understand what it means to be someone who in some way is set apart: because of queerness, or race, or disability, or one of the dozen other ways society has decided that people do not wholly fit in.

And those ways can be small as well as large. I watched my friends in high school and college realize that they were *different* in some significant way. Some came out of the closet, like Andrew. Others realized that they had no desire to get married and/or have kids and/or become doctors or lawyers. I recall one friend struggling to accept that they were not going to go to college, thus not fulfilling their parents' dream.[44] These revelations of self can seem obvious or inevitable in retrospect, but in the moment, at thirteen or twenty-three, they are painful and terrifying unknowns.

Our adolescent definitions of self can also be sort of ridiculous, if also entirely sincere. For example, I'm fairly sure I was the only person who liked David Bowie in all of Johnstown, Pennsylvania, circa 1990. I definitely was the only person taking *David Bowie's Serious Moonlight* out at the Cambria County Library. I'm certain, because a librarian told me I was.[45] What a strange territory to stake out as mine, but I was proud of it, even its apparent singularity.

Of course, this can't be precisely true. Somewhere in that town, someone else was blasting *Ziggy Stardust*. But, for all intents and purposes, it was *functionally* true, so far as my small life reached. My classmates were into Duran Duran and Bon Jovi. My friends played Rush. My family loved folk music and the Oak Ridge Boys. While I liked all of those artists and genres,[46] I was alone in my fondness for "Heroes" and "Fame," and that was wonderful, but also lonely.

Things are better now, in some ways, not just for teenage Bowie fans located outside Pittsburgh, but in general. The internet helps, allowing people to find their tribe earlier. I derived a lot of my sense of self from being different, but it's

---

44   Instead, they became a construction foreman, making three times what I do, and actually know how to set their own thermostat.

45   In remembering this formative-for-me book, I realized that the CCL system must have decommissioned it years ago, and I felt a pang of guilt that I hadn't rescued it. I hope it ended up in a good used bookstore somewhere!

46   This is a lie. I can't stand Rush.

nice to befriend people who get you, and the internet facilitates that (albeit for ill as well as good, I know).

As the kind of person who saw no reason why David Bowie couldn't be a role model for me, despite the immense gap between us in coolness, physical attractiveness, and talent, I don't think I properly understood how much representation mattered when I was a teenager. Mindy Kaling has that great line about how her parents raised her to have the self-confidence of a mediocre white man. I similarly felt empowered to take my role models wherever I found them, often in the many, many white men American culture revered. While the fit wasn't terrific, I could still wear those suits, you know?

It wasn't until I started to begin seeing people like me—and not just people who I wanted to be like—that I got it. It was surprisingly late into my adult life that I looked past all those dudes, actually, and I do still find my mentors in strange places, I guess. A few years ago, Andrew suggested I read the middle-grade book *Wonder*, by R. J. Palacio. His nieces and nephews had loved it, as had he, and he thought I would, too, since it was about a little boy with a hearing impairment (along with several other profound disabilities). So I ordered it up from the library.

It is indeed a wonderful book, and I loved reading it, but I almost lost my mind when I came to the moment in the plot when the main character loses his hearing aids.[47] It's hard for me to accurately describe how I felt during this section, but *a wild desire to plunge into a fictional world and find that little boy's very expensive hearing aids, while at the same time somehow welding my own aids into my ears so that they can never, ever, ever, be lost*

---

47   HE EVENTUALLY GETS THEM BACK. Important to note that.

comes close. If I lose my hearing aids, or if they break, I lose not only what I feel comfortable calling a gargantuan sum of money but also my ability to interact (so-called) normally with the world. I'm plunged back into near silence. My disability, held at bay and almost unnoticeable at times, comes roaring back. My difference is revealed.

Reading that passage in *Wonder*, I was, as the kids say, shook. Represented, too, in a very specific way, magically connected to a little boy who doesn't actually exist but somehow showed me what it was like to be me: we had the same constant anxieties, fears, and pleasures. I suddenly understood the joy I've seen in my students, that unbidden response to finding someone like them in a book, to suddenly exist. Like Carla, I really did feel I'd met one of my best friends at the library.

Since then, I often find myself thinking about what it might have been like to have been able to read *Wonder* at twelve. Helpful, I think. A little scary, too, since I was dead set against wearing hearing aids for much of my youth. It's strange to say that a book made me more empathetic to my childhood self, but it did. Perhaps what I want even more is to be able to give that book to my friends and teachers and all of the other adults who couldn't remember that I was a hearing-impaired twelve-year-old.

I'm converted. It's lovely to find ways to relate to whatever one reads, but feeling represented by a book's characters, well, that is truly something special, the *ne plus ultra* of feeling less alone. Like Carla, I've found many friends at the library. It hurts my heart to know some people don't see the value in the novels she loved. Despite their efforts to ban various books, I don't think they will succeed, because once you've read your *Wonder*, you won't accept anything less. Having seen yourself in a book, you're different—represented, presented, less alone—and, moreover, you want the same for others, for everyone, too.

TO SEE OURSELVES ACROSS TIME

I've been in the teaching biz for over twenty years, long enough to know that you never put money on a group of students liking anything, ever. I have seen classrooms inexplicably turn irate at being offered homemade cookies, and once a young man chastised me for letting the class out five minutes early,[48] so I most certainly would never have bet even a nickel on a group of tenth-grade girls in Rockaway Park, Queens, finishing, let alone liking, let alone deeply connecting with, Charlotte Brontë's 1847 novel, *Jane Eyre*. But, somehow, they did. Over a decade later, it still baffles and delights me.

If I was so dubious, why did I even teach my early-twenty-first century Stella girls *Jane Eyre*, a book about the sad childhood and tumultuous early adulthood of a very plain early-nineteenth-century English girl who almost certainly did not wear bikini tops and door-knocker earrings? A great question, especially since I, myself, had never read *Jane Eyre*.

---

48 He felt he wasn't getting his money's worth.

I mean, I had heard of *Jane Eyre*. I had maybe even seen a movie adaptation. But I had not read it.

As you probably have grasped by now, I did not have a spectacular high-school English education. Rather, I had the high-school English education of someone who matriculated in the late 1970s instead of in 1992, the year I actually graduated. The most recently published novel I read in high-school English was John Knowles's *A Separate Peace*, which came out in 1959. Everything else we read dated back to the early twentieth-century or before, and while I know that *Jane Eyre* meets that criteria, it was written by a woman, which rendered it ineligible. We only read books (and plays)[49] by men. Alas. My school district, intent on sending us to college to study real subjects like medicine and engineering, certainly didn't prioritize buying new classroom sets of books. We had enough copies of *A Separate Peace*, so *A Separate Peace* is what we read.

Which, adjacently, is also why I taught *Jane Eyre* to my tenth-grade honors English class at Stella. Our little school on the beach also didn't have the money to buy lots of new books to teach, and I was the youngest and newest teacher in my department, so I got last pick of the sets we did have. It was down to *Jane Eyre* or *Ethan Frome*, and if you, like me, have read *Ethan Frome*,[50] you understand why I went with anything else.

At the time, I thought assigned novels, especially old as-

---

49   We did read some poems by women because poems are acceptable for delicate lady hands to write, I guess, between changing diapers and baking bread or whatever.

50   I read it on my own, for a school book report, mostly because it was written by a woman and I wanted to make a point, ahem! I don't think I converted my teacher to feminism with that act alone, alas.

signed novels, were almost supposed to be boring. That's
certainly what my own education had taught me, as I have
explained. *A Separate Peace* isn't a bad book, and I suppose I
vaguely related to the teenage angst within it, although I was
not a boy in a prep school who kinda murdered my best friend.
But it was pretty boring, at least compared to *David Bowie's
Serious Moonlight*.[51] I expected nothing better from *Jane Eyre*.

It was an unusually cold fall in New York that year, as
if the city had contracted to provide the appropriate atmo-
sphere for *Jane Eyre*, which I read on my commute to school.
I'll forever associate the cold British winds that Jane endures
with the autumnal chill setting in at the Broad Channel stop
of the Far Rockaway-bound A train. There cannot be two
more different places than an unheated nineteenth-century
school for girls in Northern England and the hue and cry of
a twenty-first-century Queens subway station, but the connection is within me, forever: a girl on a great adventure,
spiked with unease and uncertainty, the howling November
winds acreepin'.

I came away flabbergasted at what I had read. If it's been
years since you read *Jane Eyre*, or if you have never gotten
around to it, I think the technical term for it is *a trip*. There
are so many aspects of the book that are not what we are
poised to expect, what with it being a classic and all.[52] It's in
the first person (the voice of Jane); recollect the most famous
line in the book, "Reader, I married him." There's direct ad-

---

51 I'm just remembering now how often Mick Jagger pops up in *Serious
Moonlight*. More books should have Mick Jagger popping in.

52 As it turns out, classics are often not boring and are very often innovative
and compelling. Huh!

dress to the reader, obviously, too. It's the rarest of genres, at least before 1950, a bildungsroman about a young woman. (A *bildungsroman*, a word which you should definitely learn how to say and work into conversation as often as possible, is a book that focuses on a character's life from childhood to adulthood, looking at their moral and emotional development.) Also, there's an entire section of *Jane Eyre* that no one seems to talk about, when Jane runs away from Mr. Rochester (and his wife [!!!]) to live with her cousins (one of whom has the actual first name of St. John) and almost marries St. John (!!!) so she can accompany him to be a missionary in Africa. It's not a short section of the novel, either. Oh, and another thing: the phrase *madwoman in the attic* comes from this book, because there is one, the wife (!!!).

By the end of my reading, both the book and the relevant encyclopedic articles on it, I felt elated—it was not a boring book, and I had truly enjoyed reading it!—but also completely overwhelmed. How was I going to introduce my students not just to the book itself but to the entire world, the entire context of it? How could I engage them in this old but deeply important book without repeatedly telling them it was deeply important and old, two qualities teenagers absolutely hate? Was there any possible way they might come to like it as I did, or was my affection for it born out of the aged state I had now entered?[53] In short, how could I help them feel connected to this book? I was flummoxed.

No great insight in answer to these questions ever arrived, but the school year marched on, and eventually, the day came

---

53   I was 32.

for us to begin *Jane Eyre*. My class was immediately taken with
the fascinating but sad history of Charlotte Brontë, who was
sister to two other women who became great authors: Emily
Brontë, who wrote *Wuthering Heights*, and Anne Brontë, a poet
and the author of the novel *The Tenant of Wildfell Hall*. Charlotte would outlive her entire family, including all five of her
siblings, before dying herself, newly married and pregnant,
at thirty-eight.[54] In front of the class, I wore myself out, just
recounting Charlotte's tragic life, and then threw my students
into the water of the book, hoping they'd swim.

We closed that first session with fifteen minutes of reading
time, which I spent worriedly peering at their faces as they
began the book. It was hard to tell how they were doing. My
readers were engrossed, but I'd seen them approach math
word problems with the same happy attention. Some of them
looked determined, as if going to war. Some bored. Some
were not reading but playing with their (illegal, at that time)
cell phones in their laps. Eventually, they were all dismissed
for the weekend with instructions to read the rest of the first
part, up until Jane leaves for Thornfield Hall.

I was truly startled when the class arrived on Monday, chat-
tering about their friend, Jane. Who was Jane? I wondered.
We didn't have any Janes, mostly Marys and Kathleens and
Mary Kathleens. Some girl from another school? And then:
Oh! *Jane!* That Jane! They spoke of the fictional character so
warmly, it had taken me a moment.

I understood from their chatter that most of them had read
a SparkNotes commentary on the book, but I was fine with

---

54 !!!

that, even encouraging it as a way to help them through (but not substitute for) reading a difficult book. When I opened up the discussion, to my shocked delight, more than just my readers had things to say. Jane's cousins[55] were awful! Lowood was also awful, but Helen seemed like a true friend! They had cried when she died! They were relieved when Mr. Brocklehurst was kicked out! They couldn't wait to find out what happened next to Jane, which—some of the faster readers in the class had hinted—seemed to involve a semi-inappropriate romance? This class was down for a semi-inappropriate romance.

"Wow," I said. "I'm surprised, but glad, that you guys like this book."

"Oh, yeah," one girl said. "Jane is out there, trying, you know?"

"I didn't know old books could be interesting," another said.

"Her family treated her bad," said a third student. "But she was strong."

I was just about to move on to some other salient point— vocabulary, probably, we were always working on vocabulary back then—when one of the most thoughtful girls in the class said, "*Jane Eyre* is like *Harry Potter*. Only, if Hermione was the main character, and there's no magic."

Reader, I dropped the chalk in surprise at how apt this was.

It's hard to grasp now, almost twenty years later, how much *Harry Potter* meant to those girls. This was the absolute epoch of Hogwarts, the books and movies arriving at a steady pace, and pretty much everyone loved them. Even those who didn't

---

55 These cousins are named Reed, which was extremely delightful to my class.

love them still read them—you just had to, to be part of the high-school zeitgeist.

But until that girl spoke up, I feel fairly sure it had not oc-curred to any of the rest of us that Hermione really did de-serve to be the protagonist of the *Harry Potter* series. We just assumed that the boy should be the main character, even if he was dumber. He was… the/a boy. But Hermione! She wasn't dumb—she was plucky, brave, and kind.

In her girlhood, her intellect, her nerdiness, her slightly awkward family, pretty much all of us felt represented by her, the Only Girl[56] in the Books about the Boy who Lives. And the idea that Hermione wasn't *sui generis*, that she was the descendant of one Jane Eyre, well, that was a powerful idea. After all, if one character like you makes you feel a little less alone, imagine tapping into an entire ancestry of them. There were other Janes, other Hermiones, a whole legion of plucky young women in literature. Once this connection was made, the girls never stopped talking about it.

In short, all of my fretting had been for nothing. My stu-dents loved Jane because they, too, were young women with fierce minds and hearts who had been badly treated, and many of them, like Jane, like Hermione, had lost someone they loved while trying to navigate the fickle wilds of young womanhood. Jane's charms, like Hermione's, were not con-ventional: she excelled in spirit and intellect rather than solely because of beauty or charm. Jane was flawed and real, exactly like every woman, young or old, in our classroom. The lan-guage of the book was stilted to my students' ears, and hard

---

56 Not a diss of Ginny and the other girls in the books. They hadn't quite come into their own yet in the series.

to follow, but with help they managed because they wanted to know what was going to happen to their friend.

I had assumed that I would have to drag the girls through the opening section until Mr. Rochester and sex entered the plot. In fact, the opposite happened: when we left Lowood behind and set out for Thornfield, the girls were reluctant to go.[57] Eventually, they came around to Mr. R, although it was widely agreed that he was far too old, not very nice, and, worst of all to the Catholic girls, still married. But he was, as one girl put it, "bringing the *drama*," and that made up for a lot.

Still, they really kept reading because they were as bewitched by Jane as Rochester was, by the very aspect of the novel that drew me in: how wide-reaching and far-ranging her life became. Even though she occasionally fainted at inopportune moments, she bravely kept living that life. Everyone in the classroom loved her for that, even those of us who were perhaps a bit saddened to see her settle down (Reader, she married him) at the end.

These days, at Pitt, I'm more meticulous unpacking the writerly choices being made, for I do teach creative writing, after all (and we're all there to build our rag bags with the scraps we peel off of other writers' skills). But I've never forgotten the feeling in that classroom of students connecting with a character in defiance of time, space, logic, and expectation, and of how grasping the lineage of that character helped

---

57   I do think this is a problem with books like *Jane Eyre*—Charles Frazier's *Cold Mountain* is another that comes to mind—in which the setting and supporting cast of characters keeps changing. Sometimes you really like one place and group, and you don't want to stop reading about them, but the plot marches you on.

them even more. I truly love that reading broadens our hearts and helps us find kindred spirits from across time. And I have entirely given up predicting what students will like. It's much more fun to wait and see what they think.

SIGNS YOU MAY BE AN ADULT CHARACTER IN A YA NOVEL

You are dead.

Your spouse is dead.

You are dying.

Your spouse is dying.

You just don't get it.

You do get it, but only in the final ten pages of the book is this revealed.

You were a little bit wild when you were a young adult, which is completely imperceptible now, except when certain music is played.

You once had astoundingly good taste in fashion, and you secretly have kept all of the clothing from this time, even though you now mostly wear *Life Is Good* T-shirts with joggers.

You once lived in Manhattan, and you tell your kid about that six-month period with surprising frequency, given that it comprises less than 3 percent of your life thus far.

You are good at cookies.

Your kid's friends think you're the best. Your kid/the book's protagonist has a more jaundiced view.

You have a surprising talent that will appear in the final third of the book: riding horses, driving fast, making a layer cake, styling hair, or robbing a bank. (Note: you will not actually rob a bank, but your knowledge of how to do so will prove very handy.)

If your spouse is alive, you have a great relationship with them, even if you sometimes have to work extra hard to find time to connect, a concept you will lovingly explain to your child/the book's protagonist, who will say, "Okay, okay, that's enough" when you drop the slightest hint that said connection is sex.

If your spouse is dead, you are in no way interested in finding a new spouse, right up to the point when you suddenly are engaged to be married, which you will thoughtlessly announce to your child/the book's protagonist at an extremely inopportune time.

You are far more willing to apologize than most human beings.

You know just when to keep silent, when to speak up, and when to chuck your child/the book's protagonist on their shoulder and say, "You know I'm proud of you, right?"

You apparently no longer have an interior life of your own.

You are good at lasagnas.

You are inexplicably drawn to the idea of owning a completely insane pet of some kind.

Even though you have a degree in music from Carnegie Mellon, you think high-school musicals are the zenith of cultural events.

You are good at orange slices.

In order to maintain your lifestyle, you would have to spend up to eight hours a day shopping, but this is never depicted.

You are good at cups of hot cocoa.

You, a fully realized, modern woman with a six-figure income, meaningful work, and a family who loves you, just cannot stand some other mom in the car-pool line.

You sleep like a rock except on nights when it's helpful to have you wake up in the mood to make a midnight snack.

You have made a lot of rules for your children yet will completely ignore them when it's convenient to the plot.

There is nothing you would rather do than drive five hours to watch your kid/the book's protagonist march around with their high school band for fifteen minutes and then have literally twenty seconds of interaction with them before (apparently) driving home again.

You are good at trail mix.

TO TASTE

I have never, in my life, been a great eater. Oh, I eat robustly, worry not about my protein level, but my palate is limited, by dietary decisions and a few health issues, but mostly because of my general pickiness, which was once far worse. My mom says I used to eat about five foods, which I think might be rounding up.

Nonetheless, and somewhat inexplicably, I'm very interested in the vast world of foodstuffs. When I chat with someone who mentions having gone out to eat, I will ask, in excruciating detail, about their meal: Where did they go? Was the food good? How was it good? How was it prepared? What did it come with? Was there bread, and dessert?[58] How was that? And so on.

For me, at least, food is a way to glimpse and begin to understand others' lives, so I'm fascinated by it, in my own way, which of course means, in a bookish way. I read tons of

---

58 Big fan of bread. And dessert. Love their work.

cookbooks, fifty-plus a year, surely the most read category on my book-tracking apps. I never get around to all of the new novels and nonfiction recommended each season, but the best new cookbooks? Those lists I generally plow through. It's also the most diverse category of book I read. Mormon moms, Indian doctors, Cambodian chefs, and British recluses, have you written a cookbook? I will read it. Is it a tie-in cookbook for a show I don't watch? I will still read it. Is the cookbook supposedly by a celebrity who almost surely did not write a single word, even though it claims to be packed full of their childhood favorites? Send it on over, I will read it.

I even own them! I'm not much of a book collector, trained by the low income and small storage space of my Brooklyn apartment of my twenties to buy as few books as possible. But I do own one hundred cookbooks, roughly, everything from a reprint of *Mrs. Beeton's Book of Household Management* (first published in 1861) to a couple of the *Moosewood* cookbooks (from whence I first heard of pesto, in the early '90s) to everything published by *How Sweet Eats*'s Jessica Merchant (a fellow Pittsburgher) to several of the *Short Stack* series (which dig deep into a single ingredient's possibilities) to a small but mighty collection of vintage booklets about cooking with oranges, or Jell-O, or (my favorite) eggs. It's truly astounding what eggs can be used to create, y'all. There's a recipe for a mayonnaise and egg aspic in *300 Ways to Serve Eggs*.[59]

My mom also loves cookbooks and passed her appreciation on to me at an early age, but I think my obsession really set in once I began living on my own. I like to read while I eat (I like

---

59   This is probably 240 more ways to serve eggs than are strictly necessary. Or edible.

to read while I do most everything), but I found that reading a novel or a magazine didn't always go well with my meal; the truth is that once a *New Yorker* article on gastric-bypass surgery interrupted my appetite for at least an hour. But cookbooks go well with eating, so long as I avoid those featuring creatures of the sea, a personal foible. I always have a stack of cookbooks on my dining-room table, a mix of my own collection and those brought home from the library. I'm usually reading more than one at once; I don't know how to explain it exactly, but some cookbooks are too intense for breakfast reading, and sometimes I'm too weary to wrestle with a paperback cookbook spine. Reading cookbooks is one of the few areas of my bookworm life I can follow my fancy: I don't need to grade, review, or even finish them. Their function is only pleasure.

I eat the majority of my meals alone, so those cookbooks keep me company, attuned as they so often are to the idea that we want to feed our loved ones. I do have loved ones, and I do love to feed them, but that doesn't happen as often as I would like. So the photos in cookbooks function as a faux family meal, the elements—people, food, soft lighting, nice plates—present in concept and illustration if not reality. The people in the photos appear to be enjoying their time, and I enjoy looking at them, and my own time is heartened by doing so, some subconscious part of me looking forward to the next time I eat with my own family and friends, even if we don't sit down to a perfect porch meal in front of shelves filled with rows of beautiful home-canned jams.

Of course, at least in theory, cookbooks aren't supposed to be just vibes. They're instruction manuals, determined to teach us how to cook specific things, or, in the case of those

like Samin Nosrat's brilliant *Salt Fat Acid Heat*, basic cooking concepts that we can then apply to any foods we want
to make. Whatever it is you want to do—lower your sugar,
raise your protein, cook more grains, cook less gluten, make
soups in the ancient Sumerian way—there is a cookbook that
wants to help you.

But... I don't cook from those books. Well, sometimes,
when a recipe seems simple and good, and I have either all
the ingredients or the motivation to gather them. I can cook,
and I'd go so far to say that I like my own cooking very
much,[60] so I definitely absorb at least some of the advice in
the many cookbooks I read. But mostly, I enjoy the book as
its own thing.

I love the absurdities of cookbooks, too: the always-
ridiculous list of *needed equipment* as if readers are going to
order up a blini pan and an oyster knife before making dinner. The requisite paragraph on which salt to use is a treasure—so many people saying precisely the same thing as if
no one has ever said it before. We get it, cookbook authors
of the world: kosher salt! I love the guides in the back of the
books that point you to obscure ingredients, which persist
even in these days when Amazon will send you anything,
for a price. I love how in older cookbooks obscure ingredients included cilantro and jalapeños. I love that every cookbook has a recipe for brownies, even Éric Ripert's. I love the
tea about the writer's family that's inadvertently spilled ("My
husband's mother never served the family leftovers and now
he won't eat them...") and the mild frustration you can feel
seeping out of the writer ("If you're lucky enough to have

---

60   I don't know if other people do, but I like my work.

kids who will eat vegetables, you could try broccoli here…").
I love when a book introduces a recipe titled Good Dip with
"This is a good dip," as *Best of Amish Cooking* does.

I love the clichés, too. In the cookbook actor Jesse Tyler
Ferguson wrote with chef Julie Tanous, *Food between Friends*,
he mentions that cookbook editors tell their writers to "write
about what the common perception of a dish is and then follow it up with what you have done to make it more interesting" or "talk about what the dish meant to you growing
up." Ever since I read that, I can see it everywhere, in every
cookbook, a pattern discerned. I love it.

And I love when you can tell things started to fall apart in
the prepublication stage, when the writer suddenly makes a
sheepish case for a nonrecipe ("I know you don't need to be
told how to make a peanut butter sandwich, but…") or contradicts themselves ("I said you only need one method for
cooking chicken, but here is a fifth…" which is what happens when you promised your publisher fifty recipes and,
whoops, only delivered forty-seven…). I even love when a
cookbook author or editor is clearly cutting and pasting, ending every recipe, including one for a hot fudge sundae, with
"Season to taste."

Good writing is not the priority in this genre. In my brief
career in publishing, I learned that children's books are not
chiefly meant to appeal to children but rather to the adults
who are actually buying the books (three-year-olds generally
having very little cash on them), so if you find a book that
children really like, it's sort of a bonus. In a way, cookbooks
are the same, at least for some publishers, I think: the recipes

are what people are buying, not the text. Or sometimes, not even the recipes. Sometimes just the vibes.

Yet I'm drawn to the cookbooks where real writing has taken place, those that seek to convey more than measurements, cooking times, and the fact that the author was inspired by her grandmother's cobbler. I can't make a case that such books present better recipes, although I suspect that care in writing also means care in cooking. But I can more easily lose myself in a well-written cookbook, transported to one of those other lives I mentioned, captured in the writer's careful text.

I'm thinking, of course, of Laurie Colwin, the food writer that all of publishing adores, who died far too young in 1992. Writing in the *New York Times*, Lisa Ziedner called her "the only fiction writer in history who's known more for recipes than for her novels." I'm only one data point, but I didn't even know Colwin had written novels until after I had read the two volumes of her collected essays, *Home Cooking* and *More Home Cooking*. Both books shimmer with her warmth and intellect and the specificity of her New York writer's life in the '80s, and yes, there are recipes, too.

I had heard about Colwin and sought out her work, but sometimes a great cookbook just wanders into my path, picked up at the library or in the stacks at a used bookstore. Maneet Chauhan's *Chaat: Recipes from the Kitchens, Markets, and Railways of India* was purchased because I love a local restaurant's chaat selection. I ended up learning about an entire culture—India's train system—that I barely knew existed and the food consumed as part of it.[61] I also love the *Food52* series of cookbooks, which collect recipes from their website and thus show many different voices and approaches to concepts like, oh, salad. I find books by Ree Drummond—aka the Pioneer Woman—delightful, if sent from another planet, so full of ranching men and beef and thousands of fat-based calories. I like Trisha Yearwood's books, although I don't know any of her music.[62] I don't think I can be an American woman in her late forties without praising Ina Garten, who writes simply about her sophisticated and approachable food and makes it all look doable. Edna Lewis's books on Southern (and Black Southern) cuisine are a national treasure. I love to flip through *The Woks of Life*, a book on Chinese American cooking by the Leung family. All of these folks, and all of their ghost- or co-writers, write well and with wit about food.

But there is one holy grail of a cookbook writer: the great Nigella Lawson. For me, she checks every box, teaching me about her culture (English cookery, mostly); providing tasty recipes; making me feel a little less lonely at mealtimes; and, most of all, being great company whenever I'm blue. Deep into the school year, when I'm tired and incapable of preparing anything more complicated than boxed mac 'n' cheese, I get out one of Nigella's volumes and pretend that I live a life that involves mince tarts, fairy cakes, and an actual figgy pudding. I very rarely idolize celebrities or am surprised when they turn out to be complex people with a range of emo-

---

61   There were so many things I wanted to try in this book, so I hope Pittsburgh gets an outstanding chaat restaurant specializing in train-station food soon.

62   I bet she doesn't own any of my books, either.

tions, but I would be quite devastated to learn that Nigella isn't a chummy companion. She has written herself as one so well in her books.

While Lawson has been famous in the U.S. ever since her first book *How to Eat* landed here in the late '90s, I'm not sure how to categorize her for American readers who may have missed her PBS television series, her line of cookware at Macy's and her brief presence on the Food Network. Unhelpfully, all I can really come up with is to say, if you have heard of her, you no doubt know who she is (and you might have tickets to her latest book tour), and if not, you might like her. But I will note that her physical beauty and charm meant that she was presented as the Sexy Cook for much of her early career—the open-mouthed photo of her eating on the cover of *Nigella Bites* was the gist—but on the page (and on social media), she comes off as knowledgeable, practical, and friendly.[63]

Lawson's cookbooks are wide-ranging—there's one for celebrations, another for Christmas in particular, one for Italian cooking, and an uncharacteristic volume about diet food—but her best ones are very British. So many meat pies, so many puddings, an intense fondness for passion fruit, rhubarb, and mincemeat. I've just checked her website, and today she's explaining the type of oats one should use in black pudding meatballs. These are not foods I'm going to cook. I'm reading for her absolutely glorious writing style, which feels like she literally wrote down the recipe as it came to her, then with the most minimum bit of editing, off it went to the printer.

---

63   My copy of *How to Eat* has no photos in it! That tells you how strong her voice is!

This is her gift, to make cooking seem casual and worth-while—not easy, per se, but also not a laborious, cheerless chore. Plus the asides are so great: "If you haven't got a star [cookie] cutter," she writes about decorating her mince pies, "do not even begin to worry." I love Julia Child as a cultural icon, but have you actually looked at *Mastering the Art of French Cooking*? Julia Child would very much prefer that you begin to worry.

Nigella has her tics, as all writers do. In every one of her cookbooks she claims to hate preparing individual portions, like crème brûlée in a ramekin, and then explains how to do so multiple times. Her divinations about which liquors are camp and which are not equally confound me, a nondrinker, and I laughed aloud at what she suggests people feed their children, including the assertion that all children love peas. I taught preschool. I know that this is simply not true. But as we do with our good friends, I find her quirks delightful rather than exasperating.

She even occasionally gets me to make use of the cookbooks, as they were intended. Much of my project cooking (as opposed to everyday-meal preparation) happens when the Venn diagram of time, interest, and an intriguing recipe overlap. Earlier this year, reading Nigella on Italian cooking and possessing a bottle of good olive oil, I decided to make her chocolate olive oil cake. I'd made Nigella's recipes before—she has a wonderful risotto which kept me alive through a long bout of tooth woes—but it had been some time since I'd tried one. Just before I put the springform pan filled with a weird concoction that I glommed together at her direction into my oven, it did occur to me that I'd poured quite a lot of pretty expensive olive oil into the cake, and I would be annoyed if it turned out gross. Did this woman know what she was doing?

She did. It was gloriously good. I cut a little slice, and then a big slice (hey, the olive oil meant it was *good* for my heart) and sat back down with the cookbook, leafing through it as I ate.

I remain more of a cooking voyeur than someone who takes part. Despite my many years of reading cookbooks, my palate is only slightly broader. But my understanding and affection for the food of the world has expanded beyond what I could have ever imagined. Looking over my cookbook collection, I can't help but smile at the friends—and olive oil cakes— I've made on my way.

QUESTIONS I USE TO
EVALUATE A NEW RECIPE

Is the phrase *gluten-free* (as in, "You'll never notice that this is gluten-free!") buried somewhere in the text of the recipe?

Am I sure? I should read it a second time.

Do I recognize all of the main ingredients in this recipe?

Is there any chance that any of these ingredients are already in my home?

Of the ingredients I do not have, are any of them available at the bodega downstairs, or will I have to put on a jacket and walk to the grocery store to get them?

Is it reasonable to assume that the bodega has polenta and *Moroccan turmeric, freshly ground*?

Yes, the recipe says that the polenta should come from a "local gristmill" but, hey, wouldn't the bodega employees agree that their job is *a grind*?

Is that kind of pun the reason why I am cooking Moroccan polenta for six by and for myself?

If the ingredients are not available downstairs, how committed am I to making this recipe tonight?

Wait, don't I have some polenta from the last time I thought I might try cooking with polenta?

Grits are pretty similar to polenta, right?

Would three years be too long to keep grits?

What if the grits were kept in the fridge? That would be okay, right?

Before I get too excited and think that I definitely have all of the ingredients on hand to cook this recipe, have I made sure that one of the ingredients that I thought was *onions* is not actually *Vidalia onions gently sweated over a low flame for two hours and then pickled for six to twelve weeks*?

I have half a red onion from making guacamole last weekend. Will that work?

Do I need some sort of special cooking implement, such as a tagine, to make this recipe?

If the recipe says, *It's not ideal, but in a pinch you can use a Dutch oven*, do I have a Dutch oven?

Am I absolutely certain that a regular old frying pan is going to function as well as a tagine or whatever a Dutch oven is?

Really?

How many spatulas will this require? Reminder: you have three spatulas.

Make that two spatulas—you lost one in the A Frying Pan Can, *Too*, Be a Wok! Incident of 2014, remember?

Is there anything else I need to prep? Should I, for example, travel back in time and set out two sticks butter to soften?

Would a tub of margarine that I have from when my dad visited be an okay substitute?

What if I clench the tub of margarine between my thighs for ten minutes?

What can I think about while I sit here with this tub of margarine in my crotch?

After I make this and mention it in conversation, are my friends going to be impressed?

Maybe I can take leftovers in to the office tomorrow, and they'll smell so good that my coworkers will ask, "Hey, what is that amazing smell?"

On the other hand, if I make this, and it causes another small kitchen fire, are the firefighters who come to the rescue going to be impressed that I'm making Moroccan polenta? Because they weren't that into the A Frying Pan Can, *Too*, Be a Wok! stir-fry.

Have I stopped to consider that Ina Garten is an expert in her field, whereas I often mess up Pop-Tarts?

Where is that frying pan, anyway?

Did this jar of ambiguous spices expire in 2018, or do I have until 2028?

Where are my glasses?

Great. What am I going to do with all of this margarine I scraped off my jeans?

Do I have bread?

Where is the toaster?

How about I wait until tomorrow to make the polenta, since I am full from toast with margarine?

Where is the remote?

BECAUSE SOMEONE
GAVE ME A BOOK

Dear [your name here],

Hello! I'm sure you're surprised to be hearing from me, your old pal, Shannon! Why, it's been years since we [hung out in the faculty lounge together/went to college together/had lunch at that café near the park and talked about books for an hour], and I bet you thought you'd never hear from me again. You might have wondered whether you did something to offend me and have been racking your brain for [appropriate number here] years to try to figure out what it was.

Well, the truth is: you did offend me.

You gave me a book to read.

As if I do not have enough books of my own to read! As if I can't choose my own books! As if I need help building my reading list! The *nerve* of you! *How dare you!*

Whew, deep breaths.

Sorry.

As you can see, it's a touchy subject, but I do understand that you only meant well. I'm sure you were merely thinking, *I like this book, Shannon likes books, oh, wow, kismet! I will give Shannon this book!* And to be honest, when I see it typed out like that, I can understand that this thought was a very nice one, indeed.

Alas.

I know this makes me a terrible person, but being given a book feels like… well, an assignment. I have enough assignments in my life, [your name here]. My students literally give me fifty assignments a week. And so do my bosses, my editors, my agent, my family, and my DVR. My faith does, too, all of that trying to be good stuff. So does my kitchen, with its produce that always seems to need to be frozen or thawed. My garden gives me assignments. My yard! (If I want to stay in the good graces of my town's code enforcement, anyway.) The last thing I need is an assignment from a *friend*, and that's what this so-called gift was.

Sorry, it was a real gift. I get that.

But still: an assignment.

I know. You said I should read it "when you get around to it/if you're interested/because maybe you'll like it." But let's be honest: you wanted me to read the book, soon, and then tell you in great detail about how it spoke to my soul, and about your exquisite taste. You wanted hyperbolic praise.

I, mostly, want to lie down. You see the mismatch.

Now, to be clear, I absolutely do not judge. I know exactly how you feel, because it's what I secretly want whenever I give a book to anyone. I never assign a single work of literature to my students without expecting at least one of them to send me a late-night email about how amazing they think it is, praising me to the stars for assigning it. When I don't get those emails—which is pretty much all of the time—I feel sad.

Even when I gave my four-year-old godchild a copy of *The Monster at the End of This Book*, I understood that, at most, I would get an adorable thank-you note with their name sort of scrawled at the bottom. But what I *wanted* was for said child to toddle over to me and say, "Godmama Shannon, the book you gave me expressed my heart light. We are *all* the monsters at the end of this book."

Every once in a while, I confess, I do break down and read a book given to me—usually because it's the closest available reading material when I have to wait in a long line. And yes, it's true, I have felt that wonderful connection between me, the book, and the book's giver. A friend once gave me *The Cloister Walk* because she thought I would enjoy Kathleen Norris's memoir about her exploration of monasticism, and I did indeed love it after I begrudgingly cracked it open on the subway ride home from dinner with said friend. (My water bottle had leaked, ruining the magazine I'd brought along.)

So I get where you were coming from, hoping to hit that sweet spot with your gift. I just cannot go there, not even for you, beloved [your name here]. You may not know this about me, but deep in my little rule-following heart, there is a rebel who doesn't like to be told what to do. Perfect example: when one of my MFA professors said that it would take ten years to publish our first books, the rebel was the stubborn voice in my head who said, "Like hell."[64] And she is also the reason why I will not be reading the book you gave me. I don't

---

64 It took me five years. Never listen to anyone.

want to disappoint you. I don't want you to disappoint me. Let's call the whole thing off.

For all my tough talk, though, as you may have noticed, I'm still a wimp. I decided to simply vanish from your life rather than read [the title of the book you gave me here] or continue to come up with excuses for why I had not. I'm really sorry, as I know you were counting on me to give you a kidney/ be your maid of honor/return that Weedwacker I borrowed. It's been a long journey to understanding this disappointing quality in myself. All I can really say is: it's not you, it's me. Me and my already-enormous pile of books to be read which I did not in any way invite you or anyone else to add to. Me and my phone, which provides enough entertainment so that I don't need emergency books anymore. Me and my displeasure at being given more assignments. Me.

My very bad.

By the way, I still have the book you gave me. I've faithfully carried it from one home to the next, lo these many years, perhaps thinking that with time I would forget how I came to own it and would eventually get around to reading it. A foolish dream. But, anyway, I'd like to repair this breach between us, dear [your name here]. I thought that I might begin by tagging you on Instagram with a picture of the book you gave me, with a big *Thanks* sticker. I wish I could say that I can't wait to read it or that it's next on my list, but I'm trying to stick to the truth these days.

Anyway, would that do?

On second thought, please don't confirm. That would make it an assignment. And you know how I feel about those. Just keep your eyes peeled when you're online.

Oh, and if I didn't mention, thanks so much for the book. Under different circumstances, I bet I would have loved it.

Sincerely, your friend,
Shannon

FOR COMFORT

Not long ago, a friend texted me a photo she snapped of a table display in a Central Pennsylvania bookstore, along with a series of emojis that expressed what I loosely translated as *What. Why!? How!?! Really?* When I zoomed in, I realized all of the book covers were illustrations of pretty, white, and docile-looking young Amish women wistfully looking toward the middle distance—possibly seeking God's insight, possibly noticing that the cows had gotten out of the barn again. Behind each woman, a variety of farmhouses, horses, carriages and/or quilts were arrayed. The titles of the books were all something like *Her Forbidden Amish Love* or *Finding the Farmer She Once Knew.* I smiled in recognition.

Oh, yeah! I texted back. Amish porn.

WTF came her response.

Some people are into it, I replied. Another flurry of distressed emojis made it clear that she was *not* into it. But lots of folks truly are! These books are not really pornography, but there are plenty of them out there, romances about a young Amish woman—let's call her Rachel, because 90 percent of the time she's named Rachel—who has to decide whether or not she should marry Jacob—again, his name 90 percent of the time. Sometimes, Rachel's torn because Jacob plans to move to, oh, let's say, Ohio—90 percent of the time—or because she has dreams of her own, such as starting a business selling pies (90 percent). In what passes for the racier Amish romances, she's briefly drawn to the English[65] way of life or to one English man in particular. Such books inevitably include quilts, pillow fights, adorable children in straw hats, stern but loving maternal figures, jelly crises, father figures who aren't sympathetic until the last five pages, breaths being taken away by the beauty of the fields in the fall, and, most of all, things working out all right in the end, for they would not be romances if things did not.

If you're thinking, *Gee, Shannon, you seem to know a lot about this genre of book you're being a little snide about,* yep, you caught me. I have indeed read a few Amish romance books. Look, I really like quilting and making pies and reading about the same, but those subjects don't come up very often in the work of Harold Bloom and Cornel West. However, the people (women)[66] who write Amish romances are experts about such tasks, as well as about farm animals, picking berries, braiding hair, and many other olde-timey activities that I like. What can I say? There have been times in my life when I enjoyed a book that has more to say about the celery harvest than

---

65   For those of you who did not have this drilled into your brain by seeing the movie *Witness*, "English" is someone not-Amish.

66   90 percent of the time.

about the crumbling ideals of Greco-Roman philosophy in our postmodern age. I'm not ashamed.

But even if I read Amish romances less for the Amish part and more for the romance—the safe, safe romance between Rachel and Jacob, the romance that culminates with a gentle press of the hand and the acceptance of a marriage proposal and absolutely nothing more—I still would not be ashamed.

Amish romances are not designed to be great literature (there's a reason why Jonathan Franzen hasn't written one) or to break the bonds of narrative structure (no Amish romance from Lydia Davis, either, although I would read that one in a heartbeat). Any education we might derive from an Amish romance is parenthetical, which is fine, because literary honors, experimentalism, and education aren't their purpose.

No, Amish romances exist *to comfort*. The entire point is that we know from the moment we crack open *Rachel's Decision* that Rachel will decide to marry Jacob, stay on the family farm, and stop daydreaming about attending a minor league baseball game with Dylan, the English boy who works at the Agway. It is, frankly, nice to read about people who feel absolutely sure they've found their perfect place in life, which is something not many of us can convincingly say we've done. Jacob, the farm, pies: it sounds a little boring, but also very comfortable. The reading provides just the tiniest bit of mystery, in seeing how this particular author puts together the path this particular Rachel treads, but we never once worry that things might not work out just as things should for her. How comforting. If porn is the rapid slaking of an elemental thirst, then maybe these books *are* porn, in a way: slaking our elemental desire to believe there is one specific place, time, and person for each of us. That the correct decision is possible, and we can win at life.

And while I'm talking about pornography—truly, a rare event in this book and in my life—I might stretch this point a bit more to say that it's the way the Amish have been sanitized in these books that has ultimately turned me off from them, much as I appreciate the gardening hints. For one thing, Amish romances are wildly white, as white as *A Separate Peace*. It's accurate, I suppose, as the Amish are very white, in real life.

Strange that race is the one area these writers are precise because the truth is that Amish romances are ultimately, for me, at least, otherwise too *lacking* in realism to be of much comfort. It's not Rachel's or her author's fault that I don't believe in her: it's genetics. My father was a native of Lancaster County, Pennsylvania, America's Home of the Amish,[67] and he would have been very disappointed with me if I did not note that the depiction of such people in these books is inaccurate in many ways. For example, he would point out, did you know that one of the Amish's principal crops is tobacco? If you drive the back roads of Lancaster County, away from the tourist sites, you'll see barn after barn with weird-looking walls made of slats: that's where they dry it. Is there any product in America these days—besides, say, OxyContin—that is more widely known than tobacco as Very Bad? You sure don't see it mentioned in the books.

Also, returning once more to the porn, Amish romance books are also essentially sexless, and yet the Amish themselves, with their torrents of children, are clearly not living a

---

67 Trademark

sex-free life. And don't forget that it's usually true in the culture that the women raise the kids and look after the house
while the men earn the money and look after the businesses.
So, yeah, I have concerns.

I would be very interested in reading an Amish romance
that presents these attributes as forthrightly as the pies and
the quilts and the gently rolling farmland hills. That sounds
like a book with real stakes: a Rachel who has genuine concerns about settling down with one of the few men she's ever
known, in a society where her interest in (let's say) statistics
is unlikely to find purchase, who worries about what having
many, many children, starting in her early twenties, is going
to do her physical and emotional health. A Rachel who's falling for the young non-Amish man who works in the nearby
fields, perhaps, to her parents' chagrin. But that all seems far
less dully, uniformly comforting, doesn't it?[68]

The Amish are a more layered and complex people than a
templated romance has room to include, so you can see why
I gave up on Amish romances pretty quickly. Not only do
the basic tenets of romance bore me, for I do not believe that
there is one person out there for everyone, and that the goal of
life is to find him/her/them, I also knew far too much about
the Amish to unquestioningly read a book that presents them
as docilely, old-fashionedly noble.

Still, despite my quibbles, I would have unabashedly con-

---

68 I can't do it credit here, but I'll just mention that there is at least one
    book out there that effectively probes some of the issues, although without
    the spine of a romance: Miriam Toews's *Women Talking*, a brief, powerful
    novel in which a group of Mennonite women debate what to do about
    the rapists in their community. It is not a comforting novel, true, but it is
    very good.

tinued to read Amish romances if I had continued to find them comforting, and I embrace comfort reads for all. If you, as we all do from time to time, want a safe, soothing book to read, and you, unlike me, are not burdened by a one-sided and weirdly antagonistic history with the Amish, you cannot do better than an Amish romance. At no point in your reading of the book will aliens descend, nor will a pandemic stop life as we know it, and there will be no climate change or auto accidents. Although almost all of what I think is interesting about Amish life—the intense sense of community, the championing and marketing of old skills in a new world, the inherent tension between natural intelligence and acceptable societal roles—is missing from these books, whether they are written well or badly, you will not feel unsafe while you read an Amish romance, and that alone is a valid reason for their existence.

Well, let me adjust that: if you find an all-white setting comforting, you will not feel unsafe. Plenty of readers do not, and it should be noted that Amish romances are designed to mostly appeal to readers whose lives are adjacent to the worlds they depict: that is, white women around my age. Anyone who, like me, could walk up to an Amish farm stand and not feel a moment's discomfort when buying celery. Fear-free produce purchasing is a strange kind of privilege, I know, but still: privilege.

For other readers, other kinds of books serve in the same way Amish romances do for women like me, whether the British mysteries of Agatha Christie, the Black romances of Jasmine Guillory, or the LGBTQ+ romps of Armistead Maupin, or any of the other novels out there that essentially tell readers a story we've heard before, a comfort we humans have been turning to for millennia. No genre book is for everyone: as I distrust Amish romances, your cop cousin rolls his eyes at most mysteries, and I bet my colleagues in the physics department cannot make it through even a page of most sci-fi. But there's probably a genre book, or two, or more for all.

As I've written earlier, my days of plowing through a series have ended, for now, but I do return to specific genre books I love. One of my favorites is *The Royal We* by Heather Cocks and Jessica Morgan, a fictional riff on the real-life romance of Prince William and Kate Middleton. It's as funny and well-observed as it is saucy and sweet. Much like I rewatch certain entirely predictable films, just to be in their worlds again, I turn to *The Royal We* to be on the outskirts of a setting of wealth, royalty, and true love. A world available, and for that matter existent, only in this genre of romance. I really do not want to live in the world of *The Royal We*, but it's a nice place to briefly visit.

Everyone deserves the opportunity to read a familiar story, well told. The pleasure is not in discovering the plot but finding out what kind of characters the author has chosen to walk well-trodden paths, and how the expected beats (the finding of the body! the meet-cute! the realization that the robot does not mean well!) will be incorporated in this particular version. No one is reinventing a wheel when writing genre, and readers don't want authors to do that anyway. They want to pick up a book and recognize a wheel—not a pulley system or a lever or any of the other tools I cannot recollect right now.

I'm not passing judgment on the quality and art of such

books, by the way, nor on the skills of the writer.[69] Have you ever tried to build a wheel? It's hard! You know where everything is supposed to go, how it's supposed to move, but yet it's punishingly tricky. Genre writing has its established beats, but it's still fiendishly difficult to hit even obvious marks. No, I'm definitely not denigrating the writing of genre, only pointing out the pleasure such books serve for readers.

I applaud comfort reads. We do not need to feel the brisk, salt-air wind of new adventure on our faces every time we pick up a book. Sometimes we do like a new adventure on the high seas, but it's also nice to take a trip to a place you've been to before and admire what's changed. Genre is the comforting solace we come home to in our reading lives.

---

69 Writing any kind of book is hard work, so I imagine writing the same kind of book with new characters, plots, and settings is quite difficult, indeed.

TO FEEL SUPERIOR

At the start of one introductory writing course at Pitt a few years ago, I followed up my scintillating syllabus review by beginning a low-key discussion about books each of us had read and liked. I did not ask anyone to name a *favorite* book, and very deliberately so. I've found that such discussions inevitably devolve into what I call A Race to Faulkner: The Undergrad's Brag, in which a student inevitably claims that their *favorite* book is one that they think I would be impressed by—often by ol' Billy Faulks himself—which then makes the other students frantically reconsider their own choices to seem as smart as the guy who said Faulkner. Suddenly, the entire classroom is claiming to love *As I Lay Dying* most of all, and I end up learning not a whit about any of them except that the Faulkner kid was pretentious. So I stopped asking for their *favorite* and instead asked them to name something longish that they'd read and liked, having further discovered that a shockingly large number of undergrads hadn't read a book for pleasure since beginning college. During this particular class, the students blessedly got into the discussion, naming everything from a long-form web article about the Dallas Cowboys, to a recent YA hit, to Taylor Jenkins Reid's latest novel.

Then came a young man I will call Jared, because I do not like the name Jared.[70] He began by explaining that he did not read anything on the internet, that he was too old (at a wizened eighteen) for YA, and that Jenkins Reid was "chick lit." He preferred "real books," the kind you "can smell," and definitely not audiobooks. This clarification in particular made one young woman who had talked about the joy of being able to listen to rom-com audiobooks while driving to campus from the suburbs stare at her hands in her lap. Thus, Jared put most every student who had spoken up already a rung below him.

"I recently treated myself," he told us, "to reading one of my favorite[71] novels again. Nathaniel Hawthorne's *Moby Dick*."

He went on to tell all of us about his favorite chapter[72] at such length that I think most of us missed his mistake, until the audiobooks-listening classmate burst out, as if surprised at herself, "Oh! You mean Herman Melville! He wrote *Moby Dick*."

Jared didn't take that correction well. First, he said she was wrong, and then when other students, Google, and I backed her up, Jared said it didn't matter. Then when we all collec-

---

70   Sorry, Jareds of the world. I'm sure you're mostly swell. The one who isn't knows what he did.

71   Yep.

72   It *was* one of the whale chapters! Good guess!

tively said, "Well…"—because in a class about writing, it actually does matter who did the writing—he stood up in a fury, stormed out, and never returned.

Which was okay. I don't think he'd have liked my class that much. I have a natural enmity toward pretentiousness, and it seems like he had a strong predilection for it. Bad combo. But I do wish I could have determined if he'd ever read *Moby Dick* at all, and if he really did like it. Maybe he did! I would have been interested to know why. Or maybe he just felt he should like it, and we ought to be impressed that he claimed as much. Or, even more likely, some combination of the two. I suspect he liked using it to feel superior most of all.

That particular combination—the pride we feel in reading (and understanding) a difficult book, combined with the need to tell everyone under the sun that we read it, followed by the expectation that they should think highly of us for this feat—feels unique to readers. I know some cinephiles who might brag about sitting through one of Andy Warhol's more endless films, and a classical music fan or two who claims to love John Cage's strangest compositions, but everyone else generally agrees that the Warhol fan and the Cage appreciator are slightly nuts because those works are important and influential, but also tiresome. As a friend of mine said after seeing an array of early modern-dance pieces in revival, "I'm glad they exist, and I never want to see them again." Very few of us feel guilty for not liking such films, such music, or the sight of five people in togas lying prone on the ground for ten silent minutes.

But difficult, esoteric, fancy, important books—we *do* feel guilty about not liking those. I feel sure this is true because of the number of times people have apologized to me for not having read *Middlemarch* or *Ulysses* or *The Corrections*, as if I might take personal offense that they have not read All the Important Books. (If I did take offense, it would be hypocritical in the extreme, as I haven't read any of those.[73]) We seem to think that not having read certain books means we're not very smart. Worse yet, what if we have read those books and didn't like them or, worse still, didn't *get* them? What fools we must be! We genuinely believe that if we were just a little bit smarter, if we tried just a little bit harder, we, too, would like and get *Moby Dick*.

This feels like a good moment to note that I do not like *Moby Dick*. Let me pile on the caveats: I read it in high-school English class and was provided absolutely no context[74] or guidance for it; I was not even told that the chapters alternated between a straightforward narrative story about some dudes on a boat and a whale, and seemingly unhinged chapters of intense detail about, oh, whale sperm. I cannot emphasize to you enough that I was a youth who sought narrative cohesion in absolutely everything fictional I consumed—I genuinely think I bruised my fourteen-year-old brain at *Cats*, trying to find the plot—and *Moby Dick* made me weep with frustration that I could not figure out what the book was actually doing. Also, as I have alluded to, I have a strong phobia of creatures of the sea. No matter what, *Moby Dick* was not going to be my book.

---

73 I did read Rebecca Mead's wonderful *The Road to Middlemarch* and, inspired by her love for the novel, downloaded a copy of it onto my e-reader. That was eight years ago. I'm sure I'll get to it soon.

74 You know I love my context!

All of that said, I'm sure I would get more out of reading the book now, at nearly fifty, with a deeper and broader
understanding of how reading, fiction, and my mind work,
and more appreciation for how hard it is to write anything at
any length at all, let alone deeply researched nonfiction, al-
ternately with a swashbuckling story of life on the high seas.
Plus, bonus: I would be prepared for the whale sperm, which
is the sort of thing that one should know is, uh, coming. In
an ideal world, I'm sure I would eventually get around to
Moby Dick again and like it. My point is not that these books,
and operas, compositions, films, and other works don't offer
us anything, but rather that you don't have to have seen or
heard them in order to be a smart person who likes and ap-
preciates art and culture. There is no entrance exam to being
an arts appreciator. You can really, really love books and not
have read Faulkner.

I do have sympathy for Jared, though. If I did get around
to reading it for pleasure, I would definitely tell everyone I
encounter that I am reading/have read *Moby Dick*. I'm actually cringing a little bit in imagining this, well aware of how
I could work it into any conversation: "If you need some help
propping open your office door, I could lend you my copy
of *Moby Dick*, so long as you don't drop the bookmark out of
it, as I am currently reading it right now, *Moby Dick*, that is.
You'll see I'm past page fifty."

It's undeniable, if slightly appalling, that half of the joy of
reading books like *Moby Dick* is that you get to tell everyone
you're reading them. And maybe the other half is getting to

speak authoritatively about them for the rest of your life.[75]
If bragging about reading a hard book got you the same response that mentioning how much you like Andy Warhol's
Sleep—that is, a vague, unfocused smile and a deliberate if
subtle edging away—we would be less excited about reading
hard books. But no, the response of others to book brags is
usually a sort of an abashment, as they acknowledge that we
must be their reading superior. We slightly enjoy summon-
ing up that response. Doing this isn't very nice, but our egos
like it, nonetheless.

For all that I have thrown poor Jared under the bus—
have I mentioned that he was wearing a T-shirt with a Latin
phrase on it, by the way?—I see myself in him. Many of us
bookworms have been Jared, using our reading history to
feel superior, especially in moments of high anxiety, such as
introducing yourself to your new classmates and your professor, who you might hope to impress, and who you feel almost
certain is smarter than you.[76]

In fact, being pretentious about books might be a recurrent condition for those of us who consider ourselves
capital-*R* Readers, of a fandom that's not just for a particular
author, book, series, or genre, but of Reading as a lifestyle.
We are the people who brag about how many books we read
in a year, who say things like "Oh, I barely watch TV, I usually just read" and who will find literally any opportunity to
work the fact that we've read *Infinite Jest*, in its entirety, into
any conversation.

---

75   I...may have talked myself into rereading *Moby Dick* here?

76   Or you might think that since she's a lady, she can't be too bright anyway.
     Either happens all the time! Teaching is fun!

In my late teens and early twenties, I was particularly committed to the *I don't watch TV* bit. This was something a lot of earnest and intellectual or pseudointellectual celebrities used to say at the time, and I copied them, despite the fact that it was a complete lie.[77] I absolutely loved television and watched plenty of it (and I continue to do so). I mean, we were not have-the-TV-on-all-day people, and my parents were close moderators of what I was allowed to watch compared to many of my peers, but I was hardly only tuning in for the latest episode of PBS's *The MacNeil/Lehrer NewsHour* and nothing else. My brain was rotting from within from all of the MTV I watched. And while it was technically true that I didn't watch TV for much of my summers, that was only because I worked at a sleepaway camp where none was available. I read at camp, sure, but not more than I sat around after lights-out with the rest of the staff and debated the best methods for making armpit farts. I just wanted to be someone who was widely agreed to be very smart, and that seemed to mean publicly dissing my very good friend, television. Sorry, little buddy.

I bet I was a little irritating at the time, but I was seventeen. Everyone is faintly irritating in some way at that age. In retrospect, I feel fondly toward that pretentious little seventeen-year-old reader, the one who insisted on reading Martin Marty's *Pilgrims in Their Own Land: 500 Years of Religion in America* for a school assignment that intended for us to read a fifty-page paperback biography of a famous American from the school library and write a two-page book report. I

---

77   Love you forever, Michael Stipe, but you definitely said this.

was trying so hard. I'm sure I pulled the *Oh, you haven't read it yet? Oh, you should* thing. If I squint, and forget about the T-shirt, I can see that Jared and I were a lot alike.

During my first few years at Pitt, I worked in the Student-Athlete Tutoring Center on campus, helping a lot of extremely amiable football players with their assigned essays. What I found most striking about them—besides the fact that they made 5'8" me feel short—was that they seemed to be at such ease with themselves, entirely comfortable in their own bodies, and with asking for help. And why not: they were respected, even lauded, around campus. I don't mean to be ridiculous, as I know that plenty of people judged them as dumb simply because they were football players, but for the most part, they seemed content in their skin. That ease of self, I think that's what Jared and the rest of us readers are trying to attain: we long to be respected just as we are, for what we do well.

So it's no wonder that we try to use our status as readers of difficult books to feel superior. In a world that insists that smart people read hard books, of course we want to assert that we have done exactly that, so we must be smart. The smartest. No one can be as smart as we are.

Two main problems here. The first is that this makes other people feel bad. Like the girl who listened (strike one) to supposedly easier books (strike two) and didn't even realize she was leaving herself open to being eviscerated by admitting so (she's out). When people are made to feel this way, they stop reading, and that is not good for them or for the world.

But the second problem is worse. I'd suggest that the real damage of using books and reading to feel superior isn't what you do to others—although, again noting that the class was happier without Jared around than they were when he was present, so much so that at the end of the semester, another student, out of the blue, announced, without any context, "I'm glad that guy left," and everyone nodded in agreement, still annoyed by him *fourteen weeks later.* No, the real damage is what our superiority does to us, ourselves, as readers.

If we start thinking of ourselves as someone who can read and appreciate a specific kind of challenging book, then, somehow, for reasons we can't quite name, we begin to think that we should only read that kind of book, or a specific author, or even works created by a certain author at a particular point in their career, like a friend of mine who only read midcareer Philip Roth for a bit and thus spent the early 2010s with a gray cloud hanging over his head because of the misanthropic dourness of those novels.

It gets worse. When we read to feel superior, we begin to think there's something wrong with us if we don't read or like so-called important books, that we have failed as readers and therefore may as well stop. And worst of all, we may have gotten the impression that reading ought to be a skill that we should be constantly improving, with each book read more challenging than the one before, like an endless uphill slog culminating in something akin to reading metaphysical blank verse in the original German when we're eighty-five. Eventually we're convinced that if we're reading for the pleasure of reading—not to feel superior but to merely enjoy a book—we're not perfecting ourselves, and thus, we've failed as readers.

I've painted an outlandishly grim picture here, I know, but even the mildest form of this kind of thinking is terrible, if you, like me, think that anything that takes away our joy in reading is damaging. I recall bumping into a colleague at the campus library at a college where I briefly worked. She seemed agitated when I greeted her and soon hustled away, leaving me perplexed as I sat down in the chair she had abandoned at the periodical reading table. It was only then that I realized she had been reading the latest issue of *Better Homes and Gardens*. I genuinely think she was embarrassed to be caught reading such a thing, a long-running magazine of classy photos and house-hold tips.[78] She had fled as if I'd caught her reading *Hustler*.

We academics are particularly susceptible to the idea that reading should not ever be for pleasure. But I do think it pre-vails elsewhere as well, at least judging from the number of times nonacademic people have apologized to me for not read-ing works more challenging, more hip, or more esteemed.[79] And sure, if they would like to do so, why not? A lot of smart people really like *Moby Dick*. But we've got to stop tying our egos, our sense of superiority to our reading list.

Imagine if Jared had taken his correction with a smile—*Oh my God,* he might have said, *I can't believe I said Nathaniel Hawthorne. I was trying too hard!* You might think this unlikely, but I've seen college students laugh at themselves, and it lifts the entire room, transforming it into a place where it's okay to make a mistake. That's a very good vibe for learning. A good laugh can ease so much anxiety, wipe away that claw-ing desire to make it to the top of the reading mountain, the best, most superior, reader of them all.

---

78   I adore *Better Homes and Gardens* and was at the periodical table to read *Entertainment Weekly* anyway.

79   Let me declare here: I do not care if you read *Hustler*. I'm just happy you're reading.

But we don't value that laughter enough. We're taught not to, which is strange to me because many classic books are quite funny, at least in parts. I'm not holding up the canon, such as it is, as superior, but those works do tend to be seen as the most difficult and challenging to read and understand, especially as we move further decades away from their publication. (Shakespeare, who hasn't given us anything new since 1616, the slacker, is getting harder and harder to teach, read, and understand.) Austen and Dickens are very funny, *Infinite Jest* is funny, and I'm reliably told by people who would know that *Ulysses* is, too, in its way. But the humor is missed—readers don't know to look for it, and teachers don't point it out (often because it's scatological or sexual, big no-no's at the secondary level), and the seriousness of the tome weighs heavier on the reader.

As a humor writer, I hate that we're led to incorrectly think that reading, *real* reading, the kind of reading that does us some good, must always be a serious business—no laughs, no fun, and certainly no reading anything except that which is about the weightiest topics: death, communism, and male potency, or lack thereof. (Yeah, you caught me. I've read a little Philip Roth, too.) I'm not against serious books on serious topics—not at all. But I believe that the vast, non-Jared majority will be more likely to read if there's a hint of joy, a joke, some hope, maybe a good recipe, a sweetness, some lightness, or perhaps just a gentleness of vision when they do so.

Really, why can't reading be fun? I think it can. It's *nice* to while away part of your lunch hour reading about the new kinds of roses developed in the *Better Homes and Gardens* test garden in Iowa. But only if we don't derive part of our ego from being the kind of person who not only doesn't watch

TV, doesn't read popular fiction, and has a favorite chapter of *Moby Dick* but who also feels that others who don't feel as he does are his inferiors.

However, no matter how punishingly superior people like Jared may be, my true sorrow for him and his ilk is that they have turned reading into a terrible chore. Reading to feel superior makes reading a slog toward lowered self-esteem, because we often hate the books we think we're supposed to love, and then start to sorta hate reading at all, because it's that awful mix of difficult but also unrewarding. And then reading becomes something we do to say we have done it, like the elliptical at the gym. No one really enjoys the elliptical. People find reasons to avoid it.

Reading should be precisely the opposite: empowering. Not that every book we read should be self-help-y and full of mottos,[80] but reading should fill up the old brain hole and our hearts, too—consoling, educating, entertaining us, providing succor against life's perpetual storms. What if we read what we liked and talked about that? What if we approached other readers with the genuine desire to know what they've read that had meaning to them, even if we don't initially think much of their choices? What if we only brag about our own reading in order to share a book we loved? And yes, it definitely can be *Moby Dick*.

At the end of one of my MFA classes, our professor asked us to bring in a copy of a book that had meaning to us, and we did a sort of Secret Santa exchange with them. I don't remember the book I brought or the book I went home with, but I do

---

80   Not that I don't love a good motto. *Carpe diem!*

remember the faces of all of my classmates, trying to explain why they loved the particular book that they had brought in: all of those glowing faces, some of the most articulate people I'd ever met left stumbling for words. Most ended with something like "I just loved it. I hope you will, too." The humility of what they said has stayed with me, far more than any jostling we all must have done in class, determined to claim the best insight, the most superior read of all the works we read that semester.

By the way, I ran into the audiobook-listening student on campus a few semesters after she was in my class. Audiobooks had not come up again during our time together, and so I was surprised when, shortly after greeting me, she said, almost aggressively, "I still listen to audiobooks."

"That's great," I said. "There's nothing wrong with audiobooks. I hope you never thought that I thought there was."

"No," she said, and now there was a gleam of delight in her eyes. "I kept listening to them, and I listened to the audiobook of *Moby Dick*!"

"Ah," I said. I didn't quite follow, but I saw that some small part of her had been waiting to tell me this for a long time. "How was it?"

"It was okay," she said. "And I listened to *The Scarlet Letter* and to *The House of the Seven Gables*, too. And I understood them just fine."

"Did you like any of them?" I asked.

Her face broke into a smile. "You know what? I did like Hester Prynne. Not a ton happens in that book? But everyone tells her what to do, and she just goes on being herself."

TO BE SHOCKED

Spoiler warning: I'm going to talk about the twists in a few works of literature, specifically Gone Girl, *so if you have somehow made it to the third decade of the twenty-first century without having that book (or movie) spoiled for you, please stop reading this and read* Gone Girl *instead. And then come back!*

Somewhere in my early twenties, I read a book that blew my mind: *The Dress Lodger* by Sheri Holman. Up until that point, few plot twists in books affected me. Oh, movie twists got to me, sure—I'm still in therapy from seeing *The Sixth Sense* twenty some years ago. But in books? Nah. I'd been surprised by the turns a plot might take: Beth's death in *Little Women* caught me off guard because I just couldn't believe Alcott would kill her off.[81] But actual *twists*, the hiding of a big reveal from readers until the last possible moment, when it lands

---

81 As we saw with *Where the Red Fern Grows*, I apparently believe authors to be kinder people than they are.

with startling clarity, upending the entire plot—well, those I had rarely encountered. I just didn't read those kinds of books.

But *The Dress Lodger* is something else. It's a complex novel, full of description and historical fact, dense enough that the fact it's narrated in the first person plural doesn't seem very important at first. But by midway, I was desperate to know who was telling me the thrilling story. At the near end of the book, the identity of the "we" is finally revealed: it's the dissolute dead of the town, speaking from the pit where their bodies were dumped. They are all-knowing, all-watching and pissed off. Here's how Holman writes it:

> *Have you now guessed in whose hands you rest? Why, even here in our own backyard, we must make obvious introductions. We are the citizens of the Trinity pit, dear reader…we are those you would not consecrate, those you buried at midnight, those you have forgotten.*

Reading this sent shivers down my spine. It made perfect sense that the dead, whose bodies are so important to the plot, would be the narrators, but I—like most readers I suspect—hadn't thought of that possibility because in our world, the dead are very quiet. Only in literature can they narrate. It took me a few minutes to pick up the book again, so shocked was I by that twist. And impressed, one of those moments of wonder at what a bunch of words printed on a page can do, how they managed to destabilize me.

Since then, I've been interested in what I now know is fancily called *narrative stance*: who is telling whose story (and to whom)? And I'm also interested in twists: how they work, if they work, what they do to the reader–audience–narrator–author relationship. I'm particularly interested in how the narrator–audience relationship is affected by twists compelled by the narrator. How does it feel to find out that the narrator has been untruthful, unreliable, incorrect? How does that destabilization (if that's what we feel, as readers) play out as we finish the book, if we choose to do so?

My students are also very interested in twists, albeit in a different way. Most of them approach an imminent twist as gladiators, hoping that they can vanquish it, by correctly predicting it. No matter what we read, if there's a hint of a twist, they rush to claim that they saw it coming after the twist is revealed. While I suspect more than a few approach twist-guessing the way I bet at the racetrack—I put money on every horse in the race because all I want is to win—I'm sure quite a few do suss out the twist ahead of time. There are only so many options in a well-written book. But literature isn't a zero-sum game, so I try to help them think past this dichotomy (e.g., the twist is bad because I saw it coming, or the twist was good because I didn't see it coming) and think more deeply about twists.

I try to point out that narrative cohesion in a novel should mean that a twist *is* predictable, in that it should arise from the plot as it's been presented thus far. The twist might not be *expected*, sure, and is hopefully not too obvious, but it should not be so out of left field that it strains believability. All of culture's best twists make narrative sense when looking over the plot post-twist. Of course Darth Vader is Luke's father! Nothing we've watched up to that point of the reveal contradicts that, and realizing its truth makes the story work even better.[82] Conversely, there are no shortage of terrible movies that deploy a twist that does surprise but also makes little sense (and yes, I am looking directly at you and your hole in the ground that kills some people but not others, M. Night Shyamalan's *The Village*. There are books like that, too, but I'm too polite to name titles).

My students sometimes want to write twists, sensing that if it feels good to guess a twist before it arrives (or at least say you did), it must feel spectacular to pull off a twist on your readers. The problem is that it's very difficult to do, and even harder in my class, where multiple discussions of twists leave everyone primed to look for them. Workshopping stories that were written solely to pull off a twist is grim work, with one student after another informing the author that they saw the twist coming a mile away and are not surprised that the narrator is actually a dog/the killer used an icicle/they all worked together to hide the body/it was all a dream.[83] The poor author realizes that he's made his story a pass/fail exercise, and he's failed. Once he has endured the slings and arrows of a dozen *I saw it coming*s (or, worse, *I didn't see it coming, but it makes no sense*s), then he's ready to move toward how I want to consider twists, and the way they exploit the relationship between reader, audience, narrator, and author.

The basic theory is:

Author → Narrator → Audience → Reader

---

82 I know, I know: the way Luke and Leia are flirty in the original movie is the argument against it, and I think George Lucas should have figured that out a little better, but he doesn't take my calls.

83 *It turns out it was all a dream* is actually banned in my class.

First is the author, who creates both the narrator and the audience. They're the real-life person, or people, who wrote the book: F. Scott Fitzgerald, for example.

Next is the narrator, whoever (or whatever) the author has created to tell the story they want to tell. In some works, the narrator is what we call *voice-y*—very distinctive, an actual character, like Nick Carraway in *The Great Gatsby* (or We, the Dead in *The Dress Lodger*). In other books, the narrator feels almost objective (but isn't); Dickens often wrote this type of narrator. When an author writes in third person, or in a first-person voice that's pretty clearly not them, it's easy to remember that the author and the narrator are not the same. But sometimes, particularly when a story is written in first person with a narrator who seems to essentially be the author (as in, say, Paul Auster's *New York Trilogy*, in which he gives his narrator his name, or in Tim O'Brien's *The Things They Carried*, stories which often feature a character named Tim O'Brien), we confuse the narrator and the author. But we shouldn't! They're separate! (By the way, this is true for nonfiction as well: even in a memoir, there's a separation between the author and the narrator.)

The narrator tells the story to their audience, the people listening to or reading (and often needing to be convinced by) the tale told. Again, in *The Great Gatsby*, Nick tells the story of Gatsby and Daisy et al. to a someone or someones. Reading the novel carefully, we can form a picture of who those someones might be: people who Nick knows, perhaps, or who he thinks will be sympathetic to his story, but not people he knows well, since he had to fill his audience in on many aspects of the tale told. Other novels have narrators speaking to different audiences: Ocean Vuong's *On Earth We're Briefly Gorgeous* takes the form of a letter written by the narrator, Little Dog, to his mother, the audience. (This is another epistolary novel, by the way.)

And finally, there's us, the readers, the eavesdroppers. We listen in on the story the author has the narrator tell their audience. We're the people following along as Nick tells his story to his sympathetic listeners, and reading over Little Dog's shoulder as he writes. Sometimes, of course, the readers *are* the audience, as when a book such as *Jane Eyre* has the main character telling her story to us readers. She even addresses us directly (Reader, you recall, she married him), although there's a complex argument to be made that the audience for *Jane Eyre* was readers of the 1800s and we're not them, so there's still a separation... but that feels like a thesis someone else is far more qualified to write.

And sometimes authors force readers to be the audience, which can feel quite uncomfortable. In her (in)famous short story, "The Lottery," Shirley Jackson makes use of this technique, in an almost-breezy narrative voice that seems to assume that of course we readers know what the lottery is, and of course we're completely fine with its nihilism. We aren't, and we're not, but we're stuck listening to the narrator anyway, making the story (and its twist) even more startling, as we realize our complicity.

All of this is basic fiction theory; the nuances of more advanced ideas are fascinating for those who are interested. But the possibilities out of just these four relationships (if you include author → reader, too) is enough to work with for the beginning writer (and reader), I think. What I'm interested

in here is the way twists seem to come out of those relationships. *Gone Girl*, the novel with the most famous twist in the
last fifteen years, is a great read to start thinking about the
possibilities of twists beyond the pass/fail potential. I love to
teach it for many reasons, but that twist, that's really what
intrigues me.

Gillian Flynn published *Gone Girl* in 2011 to immediate acclaim and astounding sales. I lived in New York then,
and I remember what seemed to be every office worker in
Manhattan toting around a copy with its distinctive black-
and-white cover. Fueling the obsession was that twist, mentioned in (and truncating) every single review. (Remember,
this is back in the days when most newspapers had book reviews.) ((And remember, this is back in the days when there
were newspapers.)) The book's divided into three parts, and
the twist happens between the first and second, so reviewers
could really only write about the first two hundred pages of a
five hundred–page book and conclude with something along
the lines of *And then things get really crazy*, which, of course,
drove people to the bookstores and libraries en masse to find
out what the heck happened. Sounds gimmicky, and it was,
but the book is also so well-written that the twist works.

I've been teaching *Gone Girl* for five years. At first, many
of my students (or their moms) had read the book or seen the
movie, but I now often have classes where most of the students haven't read it, creating the possibility that the famous
twist will actually be a surprise to them, which is a lot of fun.
But what I find interesting is that even students who know
the plot still find the book compelling.

Gone Girl really is a master class in writing fiction, a page-turner that works on a sentence and paragraph level, too. In the first section, Flynn alternates between two voices: that of Nick, who's been credibly accused of murdering his wife, and that of a diary ostensibly written by Amy, Nick's wife. We appear to be reading the thoughts of Nick as he realizes his wife has disappeared, and then with growing horror, begins to suspect that she has framed him for killing her. Although we sympathize with Nick, we don't like him; Flynn is very careful to make him believably unpleasant, a privileged dude who doesn't seem to have been a very good husband, and who takes the many women in his life for granted. He knows he's not great, but he's one of those guys who thinks knowing that is enough. Also, he's sleeping with a college-age girl, ugh, Nick, you suck.

Amy's diary begins with her meeting and falling for Nick years before. She's so loving and innocent that, as one of my students said, "I just want to shout 'You in danger, girl!' at the book." Sure enough, as the diary travels to the present day (ending chronologically just as Nick's sections would begin), Amy's life seems to change, her words painting the picture of an increasingly emotionally abused wife who's scared for her life. Nick, we figure out, wants her gone.

Got that? Well, it gets shot to hell at the beginning of Part II, which begins with the famous line, "I'm so much happier now that I'm dead." It's Amy (no longer Diary Amy), writing after her disappearance, admitting—no, crowing—that she pulled the entire thing off: she's framed her husband for her murder, in part by creating a fake diary (the one we've just been reading). Her voice is looser, smarter, and much more devious. It slowly dawns on us that the diary was written for a different audience, and now we're meeting Amy, for real, at last. Reading those first sentences, most of us feel that same chill of delight and uncanniness that I loved when reading *The Dress Lodger*. As one of my students said, "I didn't know a book could do that to me."

I love hearing responses like that! One of the pleasures of teaching literature is reliving reading the book for the first time all over again when my students do. They say, "I threw the book across the room and swore at it"; they rush to Wikipedia to have help untangling it; they call a friend, roommate, or Mom to clarify what they've read; or, in one particular case, they just burst into tears.[84] One, I know, posted a photo of the book cover on Instagram with the caption, *Gotta give it up to Ms. Gillian Flynn, never swore at my homework before.* Another emailed me at midnight, beginning, "I know you're not up, but *holy shit*, Shannon."

After the shock, their thoughts turn rueful as they realize that they got played by Amy, just like the police in the book do: they totally bought her innocent-victim act. No one tries to claim they saw the twist coming, although some do reasonably claim that something seemed *off*, which, sure: the book is called *Gone Girl*, and the cover labels it *a thriller*. Obviously things were going to seem off.

Clearly, even from the aforementioned pass/fail perspective, it's a good twist: they didn't see it coming. But from my perspective, it's even better because there's so much to dig into around the author–narrator–audience–reader relationship. Flynn unsettles the reader (us) with her deployment of different audiences for her narrators. I've already mentioned

---

84   A student after my own heart!

that the diary, which we think Amy has written for us, making us, the book's readers, her audience, too. But no, it's actually written for an entirely different audience, specifically the police and other investigators in the novel. In the second part, Flynn has Amy mention that she worked on the diary carefully, alternating her handwriting and writing instruments, making sure to line up her calendar precisely. It's a lot of effort (not to mention the work of a psychopath) but it's not *for* us. We're just eavesdropping, and many of us feel chagrined that we fell for it.

Later on, as the book winds to a conclusion in the third part,[85] we realize that for at least part of the novel, what we saw as Nick's authentic (authentically irritating but nonetheless authentic) telling of his tale to us, the readers, as his audience, might actually be the book he's writing about everything that's happened, an exposé of Amy's murderous plan. Amy, too, is writing a book, a memoir, and while what we read of her voice in the last part of the book does seem to be directed at us, and not at that book's future audience, well, we've been burned by Amy before, believing that she was talking to us when she wasn't. And then, in the last few lines, we suddenly think Amy is talking directly to us.

We're left uneasy, not just by the terrible choices made by these awful people but also by feeling, as a student said, "that I'm complicit in everything they've done, somehow." We've been pulled closer to Amy and Nick by Flynn's technique, and we've moved close to them, only to realize we were not their intended audience, and then, even later, to realize that

---

85 Many feel the book falls apart here, which makes for interesting discussions in class (although, I don't think it does, myself).

we are. It's an unnerving way to feel at the end of the book, and it all starts from that twist, the moment when we realize this book doesn't care about our feelings. Flynn doesn't just throw in a surprise, she uses her role as the narrator–creator to make that surprise profoundly unsettling to the reader.

As I mentioned, I'd prefer my students avoid writing twists, which tend to knot up the rest of their storytelling, prioritizing shock over other, more important aspects of fiction, like, oh, plot, character, and conflict. I know, I know, I'm no fun. Or maybe I'm just a writing teacher who's read the It-turns-out-they-were-dead-all-along twist a dozen too many times. But if they do decide to write twisty stories—and some of them are gifted at it, so they should—at least they're learning how to from *Gone Girl*, in which character, plot, conflict, and, yes, that fiendish author–narrator–audience–reader relationship, all work together so well. Very few of us are going to write a twist as good as Holman's, Jackson's or Flynn's, I suppose, but at least we have the jolting pleasure of falling for them.

TOWN SUMMER FESTIVAL KICKOFF DECLARED "SUCCESS"

June 28
Village Square

Continuing a beloved ancient tradition, the village gathered just before noon yesterday for its annual harvest festival. The neighborly stoning was over by 12:30 p.m. As he washed the blood off his hands, Lottery Owner/Operator Mr. Summers told the assembled press that it was "as always, a complete success and entirely necessary." Village postmaster Mr. Graves started to speak through what appeared to be tears, only to be cut off by Mr. Summers repeating, "Entirely necessary!" several times in an increasingly louder voice.

The event was very well-attended, with only the gravely ill remaining at home, awaiting news of what had transpired. "I can't wait to let my old man know it was another great lottery," said Mildred Viceroy of Maple Drive as she took off her apron and added it to the traditional cleansing fire. "He's laid up with a bad hangnail." When asked if that was what kept Mr. Viceroy from participating, Mrs. Viceroy agreed and noted that something always seems to ail her husband at this time every year. "Last year, he twisted his ankle, the year before that he got terrible food poisoning, and then there was that flu…" Mrs. Elsie Pitts, also of Maple Drive, confirmed that both her husband and their two teenage sons also had broken limbs and/or contracted the flu in June in prior years. "We call it the summertime crud," she noted, as she stepped out of the way of the arriving coroners, who carried a body bag for the remains.

The organizers thanked the Hutchinson clan for their donation of their mom to the cause. "She was a little mouthy at the end," noted Mr. Summers, "but ultimately, she did what needed to be done."

Asked to say a few words, Mrs. Hutchinson's married adult daughter addressed the crowd to mention that her mom "probably kinda deserved it" because she could be "a lot." Her comments were met with roars of approval which died down briefly as the stage was given to Mr. Bill Hutchinson, the lottery winner's husband. He stared vacantly into the crowd for several long, silent moments before finally asking in a pleading voice, "Couldn't this be the last one?" He was interrupted by the departure of the coroners carrying the barely filled body bag, as Mr. Summers led the crowd in singing "For She's a Jolly Good Fellow."

A potluck followed, attended by all, except Mr. Hutchinson, who was reported to have been seen wandering past the town limits. Mrs. Crist's new, low-sugar ambrosia salad won raves.

Next year's lottery is again scheduled for June 27th, come rain or shine. Potluck sign-ups will be posted at the town hall in early May.

TO LEARN THERE'S MORE THAN A SINGLE STORY

One of the best arguments I can make for reading short stories is that they provide us with windows into other worlds. Their brevity and their specificity are the selling points. I'm at the stage of my reading career in which I want both of those qualities: let this be a compelling depiction, and let this be short.

Since I read it in one of my MFA fiction-writing workshops, I've been fascinated by Chimamanda Ngozi Adichie's short story, "Cell One," originally published in the *New Yorker* in 2007 and then as part of Adichie's collection, *The Thing around Your Neck*, two years later. My classmates' immediate interest was in the unusual writerly choices the author makes, such as deploying a first-person narrator who isn't the main character. But when I share it with my undergrads, they're most interested in the fact that the story's setting is Adichie's native Nigeria.

My profession demands a certain level of expertise, which can easily shade over into an expectation that I know everything. Spoiler alert: I don't. And high on the list of things I didn't know much about is Nigeria. I certainly didn't know anything about Nigeria's university system (as depicted in "Cell One"), its corrupt police force/government (also depicted), and its history of *cults*, packs of young men rampaging through the universities, committing violence.

When I teach "Cell One," I ask my students to think about what they expected from this story before they read it and what they discovered. They say things like:

"I didn't realize that they had universities in Nigeria. And now I'm so embarrassed that this never occurred to me before."

"I looked it up, and Nigeria has a coastline? And Lagos, the capital, has fifteen million people? And Pittsburgh has, what, three hundred thousand people? Why do I know more about Pittsburgh than Lagos?"

"I don't think I've ever read a story that doesn't have a single white person in it before. Which, you know, ain't great, right?"

These are good realizations, moments that help crack them open a bit. My students are a mix of mostly white kids from the region, with about 20 to 40 percent of any given class identifying as Latino, Black, and Asian American or Southeast Asian Indian American. They might be local, or they might have traveled thousands of miles from home to attend Pitt. No matter where they hail from, many in the class have simply never had any reason to think about Nigeria before; it's existed solely as a place on a map they had to memorize, or the location of a half-heard news story. Like the last student quoted above, they often feel sheepish upon their realization.

I usually follow up with Adichie's 2013 TED Talk called "The Danger of a Single Story," since it directly addresses what my students and I are experiencing. As Adichie says, we're all "impressionable and vulnerable in the face of a story." She tells of her own young belief that stories were always and only about white children eating apples and talking about the weather, because she learned to read with British children's books. It wasn't until she happened to read books by African authors that she started to understand that books could be about more than one kind of story or person.

Adichie goes on to talk about her first college roommate at Princeton, who assumed that the writer, the daughter of a college professor and a university administrator, did not know how to use a stove. My students are usually, thankfully, not quite at that level of misunderstanding, which Adichie calls the lack of "possibility of a connection as human equals." But she says she isn't surprised, since many Americans are generally told only a single story about Africa, one that reduces an entire continent to its most dire situations.

As my students begin writing their own stories, struggling desperately just to get words on the page under a strict deadline, they will almost inevitably—if unconsciously—turn to the single stories they know: unhoused people will be mentally ill; bosses will be jerks; priests will be evil; women will want to get married; boys will want to go to war; old houses are haunted; old women are witches; grandparents will die; older gay men will be predators; jocks will be rapists; teenage girls will be dumb (that one breaks my heart, especially when a teenage girl writes it); and so on. So many single stories.

For the most part, my students don't attempt to tell stories about people who are all that different from them. In other words, it would be unusual for a white student to write from a Black character's perspective. My queer students do not have to endure too many story drafts written by a straight person about coming out. My kind and thoughtful students subconsciously, but actively, avoid offending each other. They are aware of bias and the broadest stereotypes and try to avoid them.

But they do reach beyond their own understanding, copying the tropes they've read: if I had a dollar for every draft I've encountered featuring a mentally ill serial killer, or a mean-but-inexplicably-popular girl, or a stoic, wise Native American sidekick, well, I could at least buy you lunch. Often, just pointing out that trope is enough to wake the author up to it. They're embarrassed, even horrified, sure that this mistake must cause the rest of us to think that they're biased. But first drafts are *rough*: we rely on the subconscious to fill in much of the story, and our subconscious throws out the stereotypes and clichés it has absorbed. We can see them, note them, and do better. And then a lot of our revision work becomes trying to find our way out of them, into work that's more nuanced and informed.

I would not assign "Cell One" if it wasn't a good story: adept characterization, an amazing deployment of suspense, a redemptive arc that is neither clichéd nor unbelievable. But I also appreciate the way it expands the perspective of anyone with a Eurocentric worldview and thus serves as illumination and inspiration to prompt us away from the other single stories we often have no idea we're telling.

Last fall, I had a young woman from Nigeria in my class. She, too, loved "Cell One." Although the setting was, of course, deeply familiar to her, the time period was not, as the story is set in the 1990s, before she was born. She mentioned to me that the text expanded her understanding beyond the single story she told herself about her home: that it was a quiet, beautiful spot, where most people were happy. "Maybe now," she said, "but not always."

I thought about my own hometown, Johnstown, Pennsylvania, and a book I know exists, which is about racial tension there in the early twentieth century. Sometimes the single story we tell ourselves isn't a stereotype or a trope but a fantasy—based in, but not reflective of, reality. My student said that she'd have to start reading up on Nigeria's history in order to write stories set there; I thought of my own semi-abandoned novel set in Johnstown, and how it would be richer, more expansive, better, if I did the necessary work of digging beyond my own single story of a warm, pleasant place to grow up.

In her TED Talk, Adichie has some good ideas for writers on how to rethink the single stories they're telling, which I'll refrain from stealing and presenting here as my own, but it's worth noting that she says that the problem with the single story is that it robs people of their dignity. So, too, single stories rob us of complexity. The best short stories do the opposite, I think: they reendow the characters with their humanity, their specificity, and, yes, their dignity, helping readers understand them as well as we understand ourselves. Perhaps even better.

BECAUSE IT'S FUN

Whenever it comes time for me to introduce George Saunders's novel *Lincoln in the Bardo* to my Readings in Contemporary Fiction class, I always imagine myself standing in front of the classroom, my white board entirely covered in scrawls, red yarn connecting different parts of my presentation to others, a crazed look on my face while the students cower away.

Luckily for the class, I don't actually create a murder board for this novel but instead begin by sharing a PowerPoint presentation, having learned that when I have a lot to say about something, some kind of structure is necessary. Yet I almost always begin by proclaiming, with a slightly manic edge, that the novel is weird but great, or hard but good, or that they're going to struggle with it but be able to proudly claim that they've read it. Then, when everyone looks faintly concerned (or even *very* concerned), I abashedly retreat to my slides, the first of which much more calmly gives the basics: "*Lincoln in the Bardo* is a 2017 work of historical fiction by George Saunders, which focuses on the death of eleven-year-old Willie Lincoln, Abraham and Mary Todd Lincoln's third son." Everyone eases up then; no matter how strange this novel might be, it can be summarized, apparently. The world will not crumble.

But inwardly, I'm still burbling with excitement, jumping from point to point of the many things I have to tell them. *L in the B*, as I affectionately call it, is the weirdest novel I've ever read, and I adore teaching it, even more than I like reading it. I'm always so excited to hear what my students have to say about it, probably because the very first time I taught it was almost a massive disaster... but my students saved it (and me) just in the nick of time.

As a career teacher, I worry about keeping the work of educating engaging for me. Of course, I value expertise, my own and others', and have methods and best practices I'll always rely on. But I don't want to teach by rote, insisting that my students read *The Giver* because I've been teaching *The Giver* for the last 30 years and already have lesson plans and a test made up for it.[86] One of the methods I use to bring the fun back into teaching is to select a new-to-me novel and read it with the class. My students seem to enjoy that I do this, as if it's some kind of high-wire act of scholarship, which I suppose it is. There is always the chance that I might say, "Oh, wow, I don't get it" and tumble off the wire into the net below. I don't know what would happen then. Would I have to start from the bottom rung of my career again as a TA in English Composition 101?

---

86 This very often happens at the high-school level, but secondary teachers get a pass, in my opinion, because they have so much to do. Professors have less to do.

L in the B was one of the first novels I chose to teach this way, off the cuff, for my Readings in Contemporary Fiction class several years ago. I taught (and teach) several Saunders short stories in my Intro to Writing Fiction classes, so some of the students who stuck with me to take Readings would be familiar with his work, which they had liked. And the novel was highly anticipated, the beating heart of whatever Contemporary Fiction was in early 2018.

I specifically remember sitting down with my copy a few days before we were scheduled to begin it in class. I had the hardcover, the only version available then. Pleasingly thick paper, a deckle edge, and no epigram at the beginning but a reminder that Saunders has written and published many other books. I felt a frisson of self-satisfaction that I was introducing my students, and myself, to such a cool new novel. Stepping out onto that high wire, I flipped past the deliberately fading page reading *1*, and started to read at the Roman numeral I:

> *On our wedding day I was forty-six, she was eighteen. Now, I know what you are thinking: older man (not thin, somewhat bald, lame in one leg, teeth of wood) exercises the marital pre-rogative, thereby mortifying the young—*
>   *But that is false.*

No more than five minutes later, having made it to the end of that speech (attributed to a "hans vollman"[87]) and then through what appeared to be, sorta, dialogue between vollman and a "roger bevins iii," I put the book down, com-

---

87 Why no capital letters? I did not know, but that was the least of my prob-
    lems, frankly.

pletely confused and very concerned. I sat down on the wire to avoid falling off. What the hell had I done?

I wasn't thrown off by the *in medias res*[88] style of the opening so much as the strangeness of the dialogue attribution appearing at the end. Soon, my students would call this "like a play, but not quite" which is exactly how I felt. It was clear that hans and roger were talking to each other:

> *A sort of sick-box was judged—was judged to be—*
>   hans vollman

> *Efficacious*
>   roger bevins iii

> *Efficacious, yes. Thank you, friend.*
>   hans vollman

But why attribute the speaker at the end? I had to read the entire first two and a half pages to find out that it was hans who was speaking. Also, not for nothing, who is hans? (There was no cast list, as would typically appear at the beginning of a playscript.) Why aren't any of these character names capitalized? Also, who was hans's audience? Was he speaking to me? Is he the narrator? Who is the narrator? And, by the way, what is a sick-box?[89]

Even if I somewhat followed the first chapter, the next chapter blew everything to hell. Where were my new friends

---

88 This is the kind of term we're supposed to use in academia, so I have here, but I really think of this as *The dude is already talking*.

89 I can answer that one, at least: it's the term a dead person who doesn't want to be dead uses for a *coffin*.

hans and roger? Gone! Instead, I was looking at a series of excerpts, one hundred or so words apparently pulled from four different books, each cited (again) at the end. I bet I don't even need to tell you that none of them had a thing to do with roger or hans, instead focusing on the parties the Lincolns gave at the White House, frowned upon because of the Civil War, and then their children's illness, a bad fever. I knew who Abraham Lincoln and his wife were. But everything else was... uh...

I remember the feeling of dread coming over me—was I hanging off the high wire by one or two hands?—as I turned to Google to look up the titles Saunders cited in the second chapter: *Behind the Scenes: Or, Thirty Years a Slave and Four Years in the White House* by Elizabeth Keckley; *Reveille in Washington, 1860–1865* by Margaret Leech and James M. McPherson; and *Twenty Days* by Dorothy Meserve Kunhardt and Philip B. Kunhardt Jr. Did these sources even... exist?

The Keckley book did. And so did the others! Whew. A relief. Had I just left it there... But no, when I moved on to chapter III, there were two sources that seemed entirely made-up. Also, this chapter was again entirely citations, and I now knew some of them were fictional. Honestly, what was going on? I realized I was now at the equivalent of gently swinging in the net, having fallen, soundlessly, my epic stunt a failure.

I closed the book, having made it all of three chapters in, and stared at the cover. The title contains the word *Bardo*, of course, and I sat there and contemplated teaching a novel I did not understand how to read to my students, many of whom were only very recently converted (back) to liking reading at all (thanks to our opener, *Gone Girl*), and I realized that I did not even know what a bardo was.

I am a good reader, an idea this entire book is premised upon. But somehow, I'd ended up in a place where, as a reader, I felt lost and confused. I have never felt less empowered as a teacher, having no real idea what I could do.[90]

I eventually decided that there was only one way I could approach teaching *Lincoln in the Bardo*, short of canceling it. On a cold February day in 2018, I stood in front of the class, clutching my beautiful hardbound copy of the book and admitted that I didn't *get* it. I didn't even try to get up on the high wire. I told them that we would have to figure out what we could together.

Thankfully, because my students at Pitt are wonderful, they found this empowering. Pitiful, perhaps, but empowering.

After some diligent research, I could offer some small help, in that I could give them the context for which Lincoln was in the bardo. (I could also google what a *bardo* was—a Tibetan Buddhist term for a liminal space, which Saunders uses as a sort of stopping point between life and death/the afterlife.) I could fill them in on who those actual, real-life people were. Obviously, my students had heard of Abraham Lincoln. Willie, not so much. He was the second-last of four sons born to the Lincolns. Only his eldest brother, Robert, lived to adulthood, although Willie never knew his next oldest brother, Eddie, who died in 1850, the year Willie was born. (The youngest son, Tad, survived his father but died at eighteen.)

---

90   As an aside, because the book was so new, there wasn't even much online discussion of it yet, which I would have gladly turned to help me out.

Saunders portrays Willie as an adored child, handsome, polite, compassionate, and well-liked, and then deeply mourned after he sickened with a fever and died. Mary Todd Lincoln, already fragile, took to her bed for weeks afterward, and Abraham's grief was nearly incapacitating as well. Saunders's inspiration for the novel comes from a story he heard about Willie's resting place in the Oak Hill Cemetery in Washington, DC. Lincoln, Saunders was told, would visit the tomb, pull Willie's body out of its coffin and hold his son's remains.

That's the kind of detail that registers, and the class blinked at me in astonishment. Having done my best to prime the pump, I released them into their day, telling them the reading was going to be hard going, but we'd reconvene and do our best.

I, who have seen students love *Jane Eyre* and come around on *Hamlet*, should not have been surprised by this, but yet I was: when the students returned to class, having read half of part one, they weren't hostile. No one had dropped the course or refused to attend. In fact, they seemed champing at the bit to get into it. After initial agreement that this book was both weird and hard, the first and most voracious discussion was about those attributions of dialogue that I had found confusing, myself. Were they dialogue or something else? Was it supposed to be formatted like a play? If so, why put the attributions at the end? That was so confusing!

After fifteen minutes of conversation on this topic alone, I felt I had to move us forward to discussing the citations[91]

---

91   One of my students had already gone through the entire novel and made a list of which sources were real and which fictional, bless him, so we really had to talk about that!

in the next chapter, so I said, "Well, we'll just have to ask George Saunders about why he set up the dialogue that way, someday, if we can!" and changed the topic. We then discussed chapter V, which consists entirely of contradicting descriptions of the moon on the night Willie dies, for another fifteen minutes. And then we talked about the heart of the novel, at least as we found it so far: the friendship between roger and hans, longtime denizens of the Bardo. We pieced together our understanding that they (and their friend, the rev. everly thomas) wanted to help the newly arrived willie lincoln move quickly through the Bardo because—for reasons we did not yet grasp—to stay was especially dangerous for children. And we met what a student called the "fifty million other dead people" in the book, each of whom spoke—if they were speaking at all? Maybe they were thinking instead? Oh dear, we had not thought of that until someone mentioned that we couldn't be absolutely sure they were talking aloud since no living human could hear them, oh, this book! But anyway, each spoke with a unique voice, rendered on the page by Saunders's creative use of spelling and spacing.

I left class that evening spent but elated. It had been a discussion that required my thorough attention, even if I rarely had anything specifically helpful to say. But I had managed to stay enthusiastic about the book and its many perplexities, keeping the class from slipping into condemnation or despair. We had had fun, I felt, trying to figure out this novel. Weird, writerly fun, sure, but still fun. I don't think any of us had a clear picture of the book yet. But we liked it for its humor and big heart, despite it all, and that was enough, for now. I felt invigorated, even in my fatigue, and I realized that

I was looking forward to reading more of the novel myself. I wanted to know what smart things the class would say about the next part, and I wanted to hear what smart things they might prompt me to say.

Later that week, I got an email from a student in the class. Coincidentally, when it arrived, I was puzzling through the next part of *L in the B*, thinking about how it was easier to follow, now that I understood how it worked. But it was also more challenging in the world-building Saunders undertook in this next section: now I was reading (still in that strange, play script-ish way) about angels (or demons?) luring (tricking?) the residents into something Saunders called the "matterlightblooming phenomenon" which seemed to be when they abruptly leave the bardo for whatever afterlife came next. And there were still so many characters! I didn't mind pausing to read my student's note.

She hadn't let go of the question around the dialogue and its attribution, it turned out, and had taken me at my word to ask George Saunders. She had emailed him. And he had kindly replied.

Before I go any further with this story, I want to strongly emphasize that you should not email George Saunders, or for that matter, any other author with your random questions. Authors are busy, and so are professors, and he is both. A lot of what you want to know is googleable. Please do not take from this story that I am encouraging you to email George Saunders![92]

---

92 As a joke, one of my students once listed *Do not email George Saunders!* as one of the important lessons learned in my class in an end-of-term survey. Correct!

Anyway, his email was wonderful. I felt such joy in reading it, so happy for my student that she had been rewarded for being brave. Saunders explained—I am paraphrasing here— that he eventually chose to attribute the dialogue at the end after originally doing so at the top of each speech, the way a playscript would indeed do. But it looked ugly, he felt, especially when compared to the citation chapters (always attributed at the end), so one day, he switched them around so all chunks of text ended with a notation at the end whether designating who was speaking or what source had been cited. He liked this better, he explained, and after a while, he realized that it wasn't just an aesthetic choice. The bardo is a place of confusion and unease, and forcing the reader to make their way through the book without quite knowing who was speaking at times emphasized that confusion and unease, allowing the reader to feel almost like a person new to the bardo, just like Willie. Further—and this is where the email really turned into something wonderful—Saunders advised her that sometimes trusting your gut or, as he put it, *trusting the fun*, is a necessary part of being a writer. His gut hadn't liked the more standard formulation; his gut told him to change it; the change released the story a little bit more. It was now more fun. (The very fun we liked, even clung to, when trying to figure out the novel.)

With my student's permission, I shared this email with the class, who were so happy to hear from the author himself the actual, legible reasoning behind the choice that had puzzled us. And the rest of his advice landed, too. For the rest of the semester, I enjoyed hearing them say "Trust the fun" to each other and to report to me that they told themselves that as they wrote. I even heard from one former student, long after graduation, that he was still telling himself to trust the fun. Trusting and valuing one's imagination is a key part of being a writer but awfully hard to teach in an academic setting without becoming that professor who insists on taking everyone out on to the quad to smell spring in the air instead of teaching. How lucky for all of us that Saunders took on this task.

The other part of the email worth remembering is that Saunders said something to the effect that he knew the book was a challenge. I was startled by this, and so was the class. We obviously thought it was a challenge; I was still half apologizing at the start of every class that we were reading the book, even though it had won us all over.[93] So to know that the author, the guy who invented or organized everything we were reading, felt his book was a challenge, too? I was so relieved. And the class felt better, too. Saunders's offhand remark made us feel both more invested in the book (We're up for the challenge! We can read your book, Mr. Saunders!) and also more capable of reading it. Even the *author* thought it was a hard book, but we were doing okay! We understood a lot of it!

As we approached the end of our unit on *Lincoln in the Bardo*, someone in the class observed that it taught us how to read it. I agreed and realized that with most books, we have some idea of what we're getting into, some reasonable expectation of how things will go, often due to the genre. Perhaps that's why we find it so aggravating when the book doesn't do what we think we've been promised, the dreaded

---

93   Well, most of us. No book ever wins everyone over.

It wasn't what I expected of Goodreads reviews.[94] *Lincoln in the Bardo* challenged us, trusted us to jump in, flail around, and eventually work out how to swim through it. Maybe that's why we liked it so much. It assumed we were smart, and then it turned out that we were.

I've truly only scratched the surface of *Lincoln in the Bardo* here. I haven't even referenced the way the book appears to be in conversation with Thornton Wilder's *Our Town* and Edgar Lee Masters's *Spoon River Anthology*, or the way Saunders brings the Civil War from the rear to the forefront by the close of the book, or his use of specifically Catholic imagery in depicting an afterlife that very much freaks out my Catholic (and Catholic-adjacent)[95] students. None of this was apparent to me during my first reading, and some of it not until my second or third. I have absolutely no doubt that after this book is published, I'll stumble upon some other aspect of that astounding novel that I should've mentioned.

I have to laugh at myself now, at my hubris, really, in believing that there would be no problems in teaching a book I knew almost nothing about—really, could I have not read a review? The *New York Times* called *L in the B* a "weird folk-art diorama" set in a "bizarre purgatory." Was that not a heads-up that it would prove more of a challenge than *Go, Dog. Go!*? Oh, Professor Reed, bless your heart.

But while I've mostly forgiven myself, I do often wish I could go back in time and share some of what I've learned

---

94 To be fair, there's sometimes a mismatch between the book written and the publishing company's presentation of it, which is not the author's or reader's fault.

95 Everyone in Pittsburgh is Catholic-adjacent.

about *L in the B* with the first students to read it with me. I like to think that they'd be glad to see my enthusiasm for the book and my confidence in teaching it have grown over the years. I'd also really like to correct the absurd fact that we barely discussed Abraham Lincoln—you know, *that* guy—at all.

Alas, as Cher reminds us, we cannot turn back time. I taught what I taught. I did the best I could, and so did my students, I feel certain. And while we left a great deal undiscussed, you know what? We learned from that book. The experience was memorable and unique, I hope, and it was also—I think Saunders would approve very much here—an awful lot of fun.

TO SAVE MY LIFE

Once, a very smart student asked me, "What book do you think about the most? You know, like it's running on a train track inside your head?"

Such a great question! It reveals so much more than asking what my favorite book is—I always just say it's *Pride and Prejudice* because no one wants to hear a tight ten minutes on how hard it is to choose a favorite book. But the book I'm thinking about the most? That I had to actually stop and ponder. At the time, I told her it was Ann Patchett's *State of Wonder*, a novel about the Amazon, and academia, and love. After a long winter, the world was coming to life in Pennsylvania, and I was thinking about, and craving, the end of the semester, and greenery, sunshine, and earth.

But if she had asked me a month later, I'd have said *Sense and Sensibility*. By then, I am usually visiting Andrew in Brooklyn, where he lives very near a Willoughby Street. We cross it frequently when out and about, providing the constant opportunity to exclaim, "Willoughby, will you not shake hands?" in imitation of Kate Winslet as Marianne in the film adaptation.[96] So in May, I'm always ready to give *S & S* another go.

Her question made me realize that my reading has seasons, and while some are tied to months for me—October means W. S. Merwin and Mary Oliver poems, sure as the chill in the air—other epochs appear unexpectedly, bringing uncustomary, rarely ridden book-trains out of the railroad yard in my head. The death of someone special means a return to Kevin Young's poetry anthology for the grieving, *The Art of Losing*. A trip to the beach requires one of Jasper Fforde's funny and smart Thursday Next novels for reading under an umbrella's shade. Whether solemn or silly, the event inspires the reading, and it's almost always a reread, another ride on a train I've taken before, but where I want to see the scenery again.

But sometimes I don't quite connect the book and my life immediately, or at least consciously. A case in point: when the news of the coronavirus pandemic began to seep into my everyday life at the end of February of 2020. I had the oddest sensation that I knew something valuable about pandemics, some insight I ought to share or preparation I should advise. I can be a know-it-all—this no doubt comes as a surprise to you, dear reader, ahem—but even I couldn't imagine what my brain was reaching for. I didn't survive the 1918 flu. I know virtually nothing about science or medicine. I've never traveled to countries that seriously suffered through SARS or

---

96   I made it sound as if we both do this, but the truth is that I am the only one to ever make this joke, and Andrew is kind enough to laugh at it, every time.

Ebola. Where could the knowledge I sensed I had possibly be from? I thought I had never read a book about pandemics, vaccines, or influenzas.

Stranger still, even though what I was hearing about was grim but not close by, I also found myself unusually willing to buy into an apocalyptic scenario. Under most circumstances, I'm a fatalistic optimist, no doubt the result of being a former New Yorker who stayed for another decade after 9/11, joining the city's determined effort to just keep going. I also highly dislike being told what to do. Thus, it would have been much more in character to insist that I *was* going to go out and do what I liked, when I liked, pandemic be damned. But I didn't act that way at all. I was immediately compliant about social distancing, hunkering down in my house a full week before Pennsylvania's governor ordered us to stay at home.

It wasn't until around day thirty-eight of lockdown, when I found myself looking for something distracting but comforting to read in my home library, that the answer came in a rush of images of purple skin and falling snow. I had entered another season of life, and reading. I'm not a time traveler or a visionary. I'm just a person who's read and taught Kate Atkinson's brilliant novel, *Life after Life*, which has a pandemic-themed section. Its train had been on my mental track since February. I finally noticed.

Life after Life is a strange book—very good, funny, warm, but odd, one of my favorite types. Its premise is both simple and mind-blowing: Atkinson's main character, Ursula Todd, is continually reborn over the course of the book and lives each life until she meets her death, at which point she (usually) returns to her birth and starts again. As the novel continues, Ursula seems to be able to subconsciously grasp that this is happening and begins to shape her story toward a particular act she will eventually commit, giving her life great purpose. Throughout, the various plots play out across the spectrum of World War II. In her different lives, she works for the British government, marries a German and befriends Hitler's girl-friend, or volunteers as part of an air-raid response team in London. It's a brilliant way to show readers the breadth of what *war experience* can mean, and I love that about it.

But I bet you're still back at where I mentioned that Ur-sula "is continually reborn" and "returns to her birth and starts again." I don't blame you. It sounds far more interesting than all that history stuff, especially if, like the students I've assigned this book to, you're around twenty and have been reading academic writing for a couple of years. History, blah, but time travel? *Cool.*

The first time I made my way through *Life after Life*, I was utterly bewitched by the science-fiction elements myself, try-ing to figure out the rules for why and how and when Ursula would die and live again. And to be honest, I was so focused on that aspect that I missed much of the plot of the book and certainly that grand scope of the vast immensity of war I just so nicely explained. I paid little attention to what Ursula got up to in different lives, focusing instead on how she died and what she did to save herself the next time around, trying to guess where the whole nifty concept was going, exactly.

When I decided to assign the book to my Readings in Con-temporary Fiction class, it was the sci-fi stuff I was thinking of, to be honest. Even (especially?) college writing professors have to entice their students to keep reading, even in an un-required class, especially when assigning five hundred–page books.[97] But I knew my students would be wildly intrigued by *Life after Life*. I was right. Invariably, the first classes we spend with it involve trying to pick apart how the living/dying/being reborn stuff works.

However, that is not really what Atkinson seems to be interested in. She has no intention of explaining how or why her main character is the way she is. This is awfully frustrating for my students (as it once was to me). They are used to world-building in YA novels, the way details of how things happen in a world not quite like ours are doled out in the first chapter so that we aren't left reading while burdened with uncertainty. Atkinson is a wonderful world-builder, but she also discards many of the worlds she's so carefully built in the book without looking back.[98]

Still, students are willing to go along with the book for a while, waiting for the big, revelatory twist, which I have unfairly primed them[99] to expect by assigning *Gone Girl*, that twistiest of novels out there, before *Life after Life*. Alas, the twist never comes. We never find out why Ursula lives her life this way. We don't even ever definitively find proof that

---

97 "There's a lot of blank space in this one!" I find myself promising them. It's true!

98 Although she has mentioned in interviews that she's gone back to some of her research in subsequent books and, indeed, several of her subsequent novels take place during or just after the war.

99 Creative writing students are some of the most easily led people in the world, bless their hearts. When I assigned *Olive Kitteridge* to a class, it took them twenty-four hours to go from "I've never heard of interconnecting short stories" to "I am going to write a book of interconnected short stories!"

she knows she is, or what she's done with the knowledge, if she had it. It's not that kind of book.[100]

This is why I have a pet theory about *Life after Life*—that Atkinson pitched and sold it as a sci-fi time-travel novel as a cover for writing the historical fiction she was actually interested in creating. Television writers call this Trojan horsing. I'm likely incorrect—for one thing, Atkinson has written many best-selling novels before this one and probably doesn't have to do much pitching at all—but it makes me laugh. It *is* provable that she specifically wanted to write about this time period. In an author's note in the paperback edition, she writes about how her father's experience in World War II has always intrigued her, and that she especially wanted to write about her native England then, noting, "During the war we were weighed in the balance and not found wanting."

It's not that Ursula's predicament isn't thoroughly part of the narrative; indeed, it shapes it. But it also feels like a clever misdirection: come for the girl who dies and comes back to life over and over, end up learning how the Blitz affected Londoners. My students surely do. Some of them feel mildly cheated, it's true, but still, they get a richer understanding of history—truly lived history, that is—from reading it. I love the chance to remind them that what you're expecting to get out of a book has no effect on the book the author has already written.

Nowhere is this clearer than in the 1918 Spanish flu section of the book. Did you know, by the way, that there was a pandemic in 1918? Of course you do, as you're reading this

---

100   Interestingly, Atkinson has written a sequel—*A God in Ruins*—and it *does* have a big twist!

after a seemingly endless pandemic of our own, but there was a time, pre-2020, when the 1918 pandemic had drifted out of our public consciousness. I certainly didn't know much about it until I read *Life after Life*. But it was a terror—lasting over eighteen months, and killing anywhere from between seventeen to fifty million people, possibly including my great-great-grandfather, as I've recently learned.

Atkinson makes use of the handy fact that the Spanish flu had a resurgence around the end of World War I, when Germany finally signed a peace agreement with the Allies on November 11, 1918. In the novel, the Todds' maid Bridget and her boyfriend Clarence leave the family's country home to join the Armistice Day celebrations in London. When Bridget returns, she unknowingly brings the flu back with her. In quick succession, she and Clarence die offstage, and then, in a matter of hours after her skin turns purple and she struggles to breathe—both sure signs of that lethal flu strain—Ursula does as well.

Whenever Ursula dies, Atkinson alerts readers with the phrase *Darkness fell*. Here, she adds that it falls "swiftly, at first an enemy, but then as a friend." The phrasing has always stood out to me, as it's the first time in the book when dying seems to be better than living for Ursula: the Spanish flu must have been very terrible indeed. Atkinson often slips into Ursula's mind for her dying moments, sparing readers from seeing the mechanics of how she dies, and instead showing her own sense of slipping away, her last thoughts, then darkness falling. Death isn't Ursula's friend, but it's also not terrible: more of a pause than anything else. But here, the horror of the illness is apparent in the description: Ursula's breathing is "harsh and raspy," "her throat felt too small," and "she was too tired to breathe." When she writes that "One breath, that was all [Ursula] needed, but it wouldn't come," it's easy to see that Atkinson wants readers to really see the horror of this moment in history, lest we forget.

Which, of course, we did. Not our epidemiologists or historians, but many of us lived right up to 2020 without ever really grasping how awful the 1918 pandemic was, and how close we perpetually were to the start of another one.

From that death, Ursula reboots, and we next see her waking up (again) on November 12, 1918, as "a wave of something horrible washed over her, a great dread, as if something truly treacherous was about to happen." She knows that her family must not see Bridget, although she can't imagine why. She's right: Bridget is already ill with the flu, and Ursula's mother, Sylvie, decides to keep Ursula, Teddy, and their sister Pamela home. "Crowded schoolrooms and so on," Sylvie says, which strikes me as a chilling reminder that not only do we now know that large groups can turn deadly in pandemics, but that we knew this a hundred years ago. Despite staying home, the children are not safe, as both Teddy and Ursula end up in Bridget's room, where, unbeknownst to the adults, she has died. The siblings are infected, and soon, with alarming speed, darkness falls.

As one of my students pointed out, Ursula is quick to outsmart death in many other places in the novel. As a younger child, she chases a toy onto and then plunges to her death off a roof, but in the very next section, she stops herself before she goes out the window. She can sense what not to do in order to survive, even if she doesn't quite know why.

But the flu is not easily avoided. Ursula tries to be inge-
nious—she locks Bridget out of the house in one life and
causes her to injure her leg in the next—but Bridget still goes
to London and still brings the flu, and the darkness of death,
home with her. Finally, in a version of her life in which she's
clearly progressed to desperation, Ursula saves herself and her
siblings by shoving Bridget down the stairs "in a great flurry
of arms and legs." Instead of darkness falling, Atkinson drily
notes, "Practice makes perfect."

I love that. I let out one world-weary guffaw every time
I read it. *Life after Life* is funny, in a dry, British way. I often
have trouble convincing my students of this, although usually one or two agree with me. It's not funny in the way most
of them expect. But I try to sell them on it because catching
onto the tone is key to enjoying the book, and it's especially
important in this section. At one point, as Ursula dies, Atkinson writes "Darkness, and so on," as if the narrator was
almost bored with the recitation of how the flu annihilates
this family. It's a hint that the narrator isn't objective (no narrator ever is), but it also clues us into a slightly arch, slightly
dry-eyed worldview at work, the literary equivalent of Keep
Calm and Carry On,[101] the famously stoic phrase that first appeared around London on Tube advertisements during World
War II. The book's humor also reminds us that death is not
an end for Ursula. It makes the other details—Sylvie clutching her dead children, Ursula sobbing in the cupboard underneath the stairs, racked at having to nearly kill Bridget to
save her—go down more easily.

---

101   If it wasn't already so tied to London, this could be New York's post-9/11
      motto.

Because I prioritize humor, and because it sometimes seems awfully hard to find in what's been determined to be great literature, laughing at "Darkness, and so on" is what I remembered about the flu pandemic portion of *Life after Life*. But, as you can see here, it is truly just the tip of the iceberg in this section, and I now see that the bulk—the horror of a pandemic, the sharp lessons of the few things that we ordinary folk can do in the face of one (#staysafestayhome, Bridget!)—must have lodged into my brain, too. It sank into my subconscious, resurfacing only when I needed it.

"What did this reading teach us?" is a time-honored, standardized-test question which most readers hate. It's so reductive to boil, say, *Romeo and Juliet*, down to *Try to maintain open communication with your parents*. And I'm particularly wary of the selfishness this type of thinking enables in readers, as it seems to bolster the idea that if a book doesn't immediately resonate with you in the life you live now, it has nothing to offer anyone, as though we don't each have our own track and need our own trains to run upon it.

And yet. Literature *does* resonate more when our lives connect to it. Without *Life after Life* working its way into my subconscious, would I have stayed home so docilely during the worst of the COVID pandemic? I can't know for sure, and there are a wide variety of factors at play, not the least of which was that after a long academic year, staying home sounded pretty good to me. Yet I'm still struck by how the novel affected me as I entered into a new season in my life, long before I had made the connection, or realized that what I knew of pandemics was thanks to this book. The truth is,

I stayed home to have my pandemic season be as dull as possible, having seen what it could have been in *Life after Life*. I stayed home because Ursula, who was never real, really died.

TO SHAKE UP YOUR PERSPECTIVE

When I taught Pitt's required first-year course, Seminar in Composition, my room was full of fresh-to-college eighteen-year-olds (and the occasional older adult working on finishing up their undergrad degree) who had, at best, mixed feelings about being in an English classroom at all. Some assumed it would be an easy A, and some assumed it would be a punishing C, and almost all were so expectant of a class full of reading passages and main ideas and short-answer tests that they didn't even realize they felt that way. For all of the bemoaning about how dull high-school English had been, they often hoped that Sem in Comp might be more of the same.

Such things are not what college English is about, at least not at Pitt, where the students are sorted into small classes to read well-written essays full of complex ideas and then write the same themselves. And thus, I assigned deeply personal works. Jennifer Sinor's "Confluences." Eula Biss's "The Pain Scale." An excerpt from Alison Bechdel's "Fun Home." And

Brent Staples's "Black Men and Public Space." Every student didn't like at least one work from my syllabus, but *a lot* of them didn't like "Black Men and Public Space."

Most of my students in Seminar in Composition were white, and the class was usually slightly more young women than men, often a twelve-to-seven ratio or so. Sometimes there was a Black student or two, but often not. Students of color—Indian or Southeast Asian Indian American, South Korean, Chinese or Chinese American—were also present in every class. But the majority were white women from Pennsylvania.[102] Those young women, the bulk of the class, were usually the ones who didn't like "Black Men and Public Space."

Now a columnist for the *New York Times*, Staples was a young Black man living in New York when this essay was first published in *Ms.* magazine in 1986. He opens by recounting one night when he was exiting the subway. Although he was simply walking home after the workday, his presence startled and then scared a young white woman walking ahead of him, who he calls "his first victim." First, she casts back "a worried glance" despite the "discreet, uninflammatory distance" between them. Then, although he did absolutely nothing that could be considered threatening, "after a few more quick glimpses, she picked up her pace and was soon running in earnest." From that moment, Staples writes, he began to realize "the unwieldy inheritance I'd come into—an ability to alter public space in ugly ways."

As you might imagine, such an opening landed in a room

---

102   As, for that matter, am I.

full of young white women powerfully. Staples's use of *victim*, or more specifically his *ironic* use of *victim*, often perplexed some, but they usually eventually figured out that he was making a grim joke. Since at least some of the students identified with the nameless young woman, they tended to believe that she *was* the victim, though, somehow, even though nothing had been done or said to her, probably because they, too, had felt like victims, or victims-to-be, when walking home from class at night.

If you haven't experienced moving from rural Pennsylvania—as many of our students do—to the Oakland neighborhood of Pittsburgh where our campus is located, you may not understand how prepped for danger the young women (of any identity and background) in the class were. They had been given pepper-spray key chains, taken self-defense classes, and been asked to promise to call the campus police for escorts home. While there is crime in Oakland, and bad things do happen, the campus is hardly a modern Five Points District. Yet these girls were primed to look for violence around every corner. One asked me to walk her back to her dorm—what I was supposed to do on my own lonely walk back to my car elsewhere on campus after depositing her was unclear. Another called her boyfriend to walk her to her car after every class. (In both cases, the class ended about five o'clock. On a Tuesday.) That this was inconvenient—to me, to the boyfriend—was never discussed, because the preservation of their not-actually-specifically-threatened personal safety was tacitly considered more important than any other concern.

I mention all of this just to give some context for the way the first part of our discussion of this piece inevitably went.

The vast majority of the class would argue that while it was regrettable that Staples had been made to feel bad, *you can never be too careful*, so the young white woman was justified in running away from him. Young men and women, of every background, made this point.

"Yes," I'd say. "But he wasn't going to hurt her."

"Yes," they'd say. "But she didn't know that."

"I don't know if you're going to hurt me," I'd say. "Should I run away from this classroom right now?"

"No," they'd say, although some of them, sensing the trap, would drop out of the conversation. "But you know that we're safe."

"Oh, okay," I'd say. "So when I'm in a situation that I don't know everyone already, it's okay for me to act like that young woman?"

By now, almost everyone would have let it go, but someone—usually a debate-club member—would say, "Yes, better safe than sorry."

And then I'd say, "But she was never in any danger. And she made him feel terrible. Should she feel sorry about that?"

And we'd start the circle of debate again.

I taught this essay several years before George Floyd's murder at the hands of the police became an inflection point in our ongoing national reckoning with institutional racism. No one in the room, including me, was eager to dig into the racism Staples lays bare (but doesn't name) in the essay. We danced around the obvious truth that Staples is sharing here, from his title to his opening anecdote to the rest of the essay, which details a number of incidents of racism he personally endured. My students at the time were reluctant to agree that the young woman was being racist: I heard a lot of "anyone following me that closely would scare me!" In response to which I just turned them back to the essay to point out that he said he was not following her closely. Most of the girls in the class were unconvinced, and to be fair to them, perhaps each had at least one story of a benign-seeming man who had turned out to have ill intent in the end.

The occasional Black students in the class surely understood Staples's depiction of racism far better than I could. Early in my teaching career, I determined that I would never call on a Black student and ask them to explain to others what it is to be Black in America—this determination is the result of my too often being asked to explain to others what it is to be hand-icapped—so I didn't ask. Besides, Staples's essay is oblique, stopping short of naming the thing, and I think that few of my Black students wanted the responsibility of putting the period at the end of his sentence. What if the other students continued to argue that what they knew to be true was not?

Today, I think, more students would agree that the young woman's actions were at least informed by racism even if she did not perceive them to be. At the time, the most I was able to get them to agree to was that a white grandmotherly type toddling along behind the young woman would not have provoked the same fear.

Later in the essay, Staples tells an anecdote about stopping in at a jewelry store to kill some time before he conducted an interview as part of his occupation as a journalist. Upon his entry, the clerk disappeared and returned a moment later with a Doberman on a leash, "silent to my questions, her eyes bulging nearly out of her head." Bringing up this story always slides the class's sympathy more toward Staples. They feel the clerk is overreacting. ("It's also not behaving badly to exit a subway station," I or another student always pointed out.)

"The dog is a step too far. That makes her the aggressor," someone would say.

"Okay, so why is she afraid?" I'd ask, as if the title of the essay didn't give them the answer.

"Well, we don't know the whole story," someone would say. "Maybe he did something that was innocent but made her scared."

"I'm sure he didn't mean to," another student would say, "but maybe something bad had happened to her at some point, and..."

And it was around here that someone would say, usually out of utter frustration, "Because he's Black. She's scared of him because he's Black. Because white women are supposed to be afraid of Black men."

Then everyone would get very quiet.

I loved that uncomfortable silence, which meant that people in the room were processing. Look, as I've said, I'm just a white lady from Western Pennsylvania. My high-school graduation gifts included a pepper-spray key chain from my school's orchestra teacher,[103] and I took some self-defense classes before I moved to New York.[104] I have friends who were mugged in pre-Giuliani New York and students who were attacked in Pittsburgh, and the salient fact that such ag-

---

103 I have a vivid recollection of someone saying, "Oh, how practical!" as I opened it at my party. I never used it.

104 Mentioning them here is the only time I've gotten any use out of them whatsoever.

gression almost always comes from a person the victim knows doesn't mean that there aren't random attacks outside subway stations to this day.

But I've always hated the way *you can never be too careful* victimizes women *and* Black or brown men at the same time. It implies that the world is always, inevitably dangerous for women, and thus we must act in extreme ways that prioritize keeping us safe over any other concerns, whether for a sense of common humanity or for anyone else's emotional health. The phrase implies a constant standoff between bad Black men and innocent white women. I am a person of innate caution and hesitancy, but I hate *you can never be too careful* because it's total bullshit. You *can* be too careful. You can act out of fear, a fear rooted in racism. You can overlook that the most danger you face is probably from the men you already know, and you can traumatize people who sincerely and entirely meant you no harm. So I was always glad to see my students chip away at that line of thinking, to help them realize that there are gradations between *I am blithely walking into sure danger* and *the only response to my anxiety is to react abruptly and with my worst impulses*. Those gradations are a liminal space, and far less comfortable to inhabit.

It's not really a surprise that many of my students, across all identities, felt destabilized by this, and I'm sure that not a few of the young women readjusted back to a *better safe than sorry* attitude within days (minutes?) of finishing up our discussion of "Black Men and Public Space."[105] But those who held on to that nuance, who could see that while the young

---

105   For all I know, that one girl is still being picked up by her now-husband after work.

woman acted out of what was likely her cultural training, it was also hurtful to Staples who did not mean any harm (he was both safe and sorry, as one student pointed out), I suspect they were more open to the nuance and sorrow and potential of our country's reckoning with race.

Or perhaps they just had an uncomfortable reading experience, forced to walk in someone else's shoes. That's fine, too. Reading isn't only around to make us feel cozy.

For all of my bravado about teaching the Staples essay, I almost chose not to the first time I had a young Black man in my class. I worried about how discussing this essay would affect him, and I hoped his classmates would not cast him in the role of Speaker for His Race even if I steadfastly refused to do so. As it turned out, the only thing he had to say was about Staples's closing, in which the writer mentions that he's taken to whistling when out and about at night. He writes, "It is my equivalent of the cowbell that hikers wear when they know they are in bear country."

My student said, "My dad does that."

To which none of us had anything else to say.

THE FIVE PEOPLE YOU MEET WHEN YOU WORK IN A BOOKSTORE

(For Arlan Hess)

1.Judy

Absolutely determined to purchase *The Five People You Meet in Heaven* for her grandson, Tyler, who is turning sixteen this weekend. Will not be dissuaded, no matter that 1) the book is no longer available at most bookstores without special order, having been published nearly twenty years ago, and 2) there is absolutely no way Tyler is interested in reading it.

2.Nathan

Heard about a book on NPR and wants to purchase it. Cannot remember anything about the book except that it might have a blue cover. Or maybe *blue* is in the title. Or it could be *blew*. Or *blow*. Or *bow*? Do you have that one?

3.Maura

Not interested in buying any books but just happens to have twenty copies of her self-published novel, *Yinz Lovers: A 1980 Steelers Love Story*, which she wondered if you would maybe be willing to sell at your store?

4.Leia

Spotted trying to read *Tipping the Velvet* in the Health and Wellness section. Has a mild panic attack when you ask if she needs anything. Ends up inexplicably buying three copies of *The Old Man and the Sea* instead.

5.Jared

Takes photos of a dozen different book covers, then tells you about how he's going to buy them from Amazon instead. Is currently buried in the bookstore's backyard and will be one of the five people you meet in hell.

BECAUSE SOMEONE IS PAYING YOU TO TEACH A CLASS ABOUT VAMPIRES

My twenty-plus-year teaching career has taken me many places I did not expect to go. For the most part, I think I've embraced such unexpected journeys with courage and, where merited, enthusiasm. One of the lone exceptions is the time I had to go to Transylvania.

Let me explain. When you are an adjunct professor, as I was for a few years between finishing up my MFA and when they blessedly found me a full-time position at Pitt, you teach whatever classes are offered to you, because you get paid by the class. If you're offered more than one class at the same university, you definitely, definitely take it, no matter what it is, because that saves you money and time on commuting. So it was that I accepted an offer to teach a course called— and I am not exaggerating here for comic effect—*Vampire! Blood and Empire!*

I did not name this course, nor did I design it. The Slavic Department of the University of Pittsburgh did both of those things. Pitt requires all undergrads to take a class in non-American cultures, and since *Vampire! Blood and Empire!* was one of the options, a great deal of students enrolled in it.

At Pitt, this course was very well-known. A number of English part-time faculty had taught it over the years; the Slavic department is small, and the class, unable to focus on archaeology or history since—spoiler alert—vampires are not real, was essentially a literature course. It made sense to get a good English adjunct to teach it, which I was. In fact, I had almost all of the necessary qualifications: I was comfortable teaching in front of a class of two hundred people; I could read vast amounts of literature quickly; I could put together a multiple-choice test; I was loud enough to be heard in the back of the auditorium; and years of teaching high school had honed my ability to stare down a talking student until he stopped. There was only one small problem.

I was afraid of vampires.

Which was unfortunate because I had to read a great deal about vampires and quickly, as I signed the contract to teach the class just two weeks before it began. And yet, day after day, as those two weeks trickled by, I did none of the reading that I would soon assign my class. It became a problem.

Let's go a little wider, here. I wasn't just afraid of vampires. In fact, because I liked *Buffy the Vampire Slayer* when it was on TV (although I always watched in the company of Andrew and his partner, Corey, so I wouldn't get too scared), I'd say that I was the least afraid of vampires of all the many things that terrified me, which was a long list, indeed: Creatures of the sea. Werewolves. Zombies. Mummies (real and cinematic). Frankenstein's monster (probably Frankenstein, too, who seemed to have issues). Serial killers. Less ambitious, one-is-enough killers. Supernatural forces. Mean dogs. Coyotes. Ghosts, of course. Creepy, ghost-possessed children, sure. Clowns. Distorted features on faces. Bugs. Snakes. Monkeys. More on them in a bit.

Look, let's just cut to the chase. I'll admit it: I was a scaredy-cat, and especially about scary books because 1) unlike watching a scary movie, I can't close my eyes while reading a book, and 2) while a scary movie's CGI might be terrible enough to laugh at, with a book, my brain has free rein to create images of couture-sewn terror made just for me. I also feel compelled to finish most books I start, whereas I can walk away from a movie with ease. So if I somehow begin a book of horror, I am going to see it through, weeping with terror as I read. I had had some bad experiences.

Let's travel back in time to the scariest thing I've ever read: a set of books called *The Universal Classic Monster Series*, which I found as a first grader in the library of my elementary school in Mechanicsburg, Pennsylvania. Each book took the title of a famous monster movie and added exclamation points and boldness: ***Frankenstein!!!*** The books were a series of black-and-white stills from the movie, the text recounting the plot with bits of dialogue sprinkled in. The pictures particularly got under my skin, I think because they made me think about the opening of *The Wizard of Oz*, also black-and-white, and also very frightening to young Shannon.

(In case you're wondering why my parents allowed me to watch things that scared me, it should be noted that my bar for being scared was astoundingly low. For example, I was also scared of the way Rita Moreno screamed "Hey, you guys!" at the beginning of *The Electric Company* on TV, a show *meant* for children. It wasn't particularly hard to freak me out. My parents could never have kept track.)

Anyway, the library had perhaps twenty *Universal Classic Monster Series* books, and I took one out every time my class visited, about once a week. The series's title refers to the Universal movie studio, which, between the 1920s and 1950s, released such now-classic/always-campy films as *Dracula*, *The Mummy*, *The Wolf Man*, and *Frankenstein*. Because these monsters/misunderstood folks made appearances in one another's films, this is considered the first "shared universe" in moviemaking history. The campiness and silliness of those monsters totally went over my head, and I took them with deadly earnestness. That basic tenet of horror, that it puts us through the wringer in order to bring us out released, that it is a catharsis, was lost on me.

As it is on most scaredy-cats. We're not delightfully energized by horror the way the rest of the world is; we take those images with us, and our brains offer them back at three in the morning, no catharsis to be found. We look at the way the rest of you scream, then laugh, and then relax, with envy— and, fascinated, we want in. But we can't get in.

That fascination/fear dialectic may be the key characteristic of being a scaredy-cat. We're as intrigued as anyone, and we sense that others are able to release their fear, a logical response that we long for but can't quite perform. I mean, for years, I referred to *The Electric Company* as *Hey, You Guys!* as if that was its title, trying to own the moment that I was too scared to listen to, myself. I think I wanted to name what scared me, because if I did maybe it would stop. (It did not.)

That's what makes my relationship with horror so different than the other things I don't get the same thrill from. I mean, I don't like wine, so I don't drink wine, which works out great: I spend 0 percent of my life thinking about wine.[106] But as a kid, I couldn't stop chasing the cathartic joy I saw others feel when watching or reading horror, and I had not yet learned that my fascinated chase would lead to terror as the books came back to haunt me later. So I continued to pursue the Universal books at my personal mental peril, and to the detriment of my family's sleep patterns.

It worked like this. I would take one of the books up to the librarian's desk. She was always very reluctant to let me check it out. At first, this was because the books were actually meant for older kids: the text was small, and the stories much more complex than my grade level, although I was clearly reading way past that. Later, she tried to discourage me because my poor parents asked her to try.

That's because I would take the book home, read it carefully—I tried not to touch the parts of the pages that had monsters depicted on them, a pretty clear sign I shouldn't have been reading those books—and really analyze the photos for all the nuances. "Dracula is very pale," I would think to myself. "The Wolf Man has kind eyes. Frankenstein could crush my tiny body the way he will kill this little blonde girl pictured here."[107] The voice in my head was very calm as it

---

106 Writing these sentences may be the most I've ever thought about wine.

107 I know, he's Frankenstein's *monster*, but the book/movie didn't make that clear.

tried to gather information, as if the point was to learn how to protect myself and my family from monsters. But those books weren't so much ten-point plans to guard against a monster infestation as, you know, a book written to give you the heebie-jeebies. I mean, I was seven. I was doing my best.

In the light of day and with my brain firmly under control, my terror abated as my fascination was slaked by the fresh information. I wrapped up my day, dinner and TV and maybe some ice cream, then I would go to bed, and *then*, in the witching hour, finally, the heebie-jeebies kicked in. I'd wake up screaming or crying. Or just scared. Either way, I called for my parents, and my poor, poor mother would make her way into my room, exhausted, to try to reason with me. Eventually, I'd calm down and fall back asleep. Then I'd run the whole cycle again the next day, until the book was returned to the library, or my mom managed to hide it from me for the rest of the week. And then, on library day at school, the cycle would start all over with a fresh monster.

Thankfully for everyone, I stopped taking those books out of the library, mostly because the librarian redirected me to tamer stuff, even opening up the hallowed Fifth Grade and Up section, so long as I stuck with Beverly Cleary and her kin. No R. L. Stine for me.

I learned to live with the fascination that I could not satisfy, using information-gathering to scratch the itch, which is another way of saying that if you were my friend before the year 2010, you probably spent at least some of our time together telling me the plot of *The Blair Witch Project*. I wanted to know what happened, but I knew I had to stick to my resolve to stay away.

Avoiding horror hasn't been easy. Even when I managed it on my own, my teachers weren't on my side. They get away with assigning all kinds of reading, and no one tells them to make concessions for the scaredy-cats in their classes.[108]

As an educator, I have mixed feelings about trigger or content warnings, but like most folks, I feel *my* personal triggers should be respected. Thus, I deeply believe that there should be an opt-out clause for scaredy-cats when it comes to assigned reading. Of course, I never came close to getting one when I was in school, so what I would usually do is simply not read any assignment that I sensed drifted toward horror. Since I read everything else, this didn't cause any issues, and I ignored all class discussions of works like W. W. Jacobs's "The Monkey's Paw," the plot of which is still vague to me.[109]

This system mostly worked well until the day we were assigned to read the Stephen King short story "The Monkey" in my middle-school class. By this I mean, we had to sit there and read it. Under the teacher's eye.

You'll remember that one of the things I am/was scared of is monkeys. In the story, there's an olde-timey, cymbal-banging toy monkey, and it does bad things, like kill people, quite a lot of people. Also, the story is really scary because, I don't know if you've heard much about this young, up-and-coming writer, Steve King, but he's going places.

Reading this story also felt like a direct attack on me because just a few days before we were assigned it, I had visited my antique-collecting grandparents, and my grandfather had been very excited to show me the cool new toy he'd found

108 Do I sound unusually bitter toward my fellow educators? *I am.*

109 I assume that there is a monkey's paw, and other bad things.

at a shop, a cymbal-banging monkey, which (surprise!) I did not like at all. Subsequently, my only recollection of the class discussion of the story was that I presented a long and detailed description of what the toy looked like, down to its plaid vest, as if I expected it to show up in the cafeteria and wanted my classmates to be able to ID it.

My just-don't-read-it plan fell apart as I got older and was required to write about the scary works we were assigned. It's hard to read with your eyes half-closed, but I managed it, picking my way through du Maurier's *Rebecca* and Ray Bradbury's "All Summer in a Day," and Shirley Jackson's "The Lottery," and—God help me—Edgar Allen Poe's cheery oeuvre.

But none had as much of an effect as Nevil Shute's novel *On the Beach*, which I read in high school. I can't imagine it's assigned much anymore, because it's grim as hell. Shute wrote about the last surviving people, post–nuclear war, who were wrapping up humanity in Australia as they waited for the leftover radiation to float on down their way and annihilate them. Most of the people in the book end up committing suicide and/or murder. No monsters here, just existential dread that felt all too realistic and familiar in Cold War (or Just Shortly after the Cold War) America. This book was not kidding around, which I assume was why my English teacher assigned it. As a teacher, I recognize this instinct, to burn something into the brains of your students, in hopes that they carry and disseminate the message long after you are gone. For him, the futility of nuclear war must have felt like *the* lesson we needed to learn.

I don't know if *On the Beach* was well-written, per se, but it was *vividly* written—there was sex, and longing, and drama, and submarines, and suspense, and Australia, and, most of all, *imminent death.* Just as my teacher must have wanted, it did change me. While reading it, I had to negotiate the flux of fascination/horror that had so confused me as a child. My analytical brain had to work a double shift—first, to pick up all of the cool details and synthesize the complicated, multi-pronged plot, and second, to keep my flailing scaredy-cat self under control, usually through a low-key but constant repetition of *This could happen but is not happening* to myself as I read.

And I finally kind of got it: I grasped that what I was reading wasn't real, even at night, when I thought about it under the covers I still kept pulled up to my chin because of Dracula. But I also understood why it got to me and my classmates, and even enjoyed the feeling, of something cutting almost too close. I felt more alive and more grateful for that life after I read it. For once, I felt the release of catharsis.

Since that felt like a lucky break, I took the lesson but continued to steadfastly stay away from horror, a bargain with myself in which I promise not to give my brain terrifying material, and in return, it agrees not to craft such material into images at 2:00 a.m. anymore. The plan worked well, until, as you know, *Vampire! Blood and Empire!* arrived into my life.

I'm far too much of a Try Hard not to prep for my class, so after putting it off for far longer than I felt comfortable with, I did eventually read the material I'd need to teach in the first two weeks of the course. It was mostly folk legends about vampires, specifically (of course) in the Slavic region.[110]

---

110   The syllabus did make a valiant attempt to tie the materials more to Eastern Europe than to Universal Studios.

It was creepy, but there was little in the way of really convincing writing. It was all like "Take ye the dill and smear it about the doorframe to keep away the *undead* and ye should also boil the wool of a young lamb…"

Thus armed with the knowledge of what various herbs could do to keep away the undead, I arrived to my first day of class as a vampire professor. Professor of vampires? Vampiric scholar? Anyway, I showed up and unpacked my bag on the professor's desk at the front, slowly eyeing what kind of students would sign up for a class on vampires.

In the back of the room, there were the kids taking the class as a requirement; they wouldn't be listening to much of anything I said, were only present because I took attendance, and would squeak by with a C− or D. I called them the Don't Cares. They don't appear again in this essay.

In the very front of the room, their noses practically pressed against my desk, were the overachievers, the Try Hards, the students who wanted an A+ in this and every class. They were very frequently science or engineering majors, and taking this class was intellectually slumming for them, but they still wanted to excel. Many of them were young women who would answer any question I asked, bless them. I knew both of these groups well already.

But *Vampire! Blood and Empire!* presented three further types. Directly behind the Try Hards were those who I would come to call the True Believers, students who, on some level, believed vampires were actually real. Many of them had an unhealthy obsession with the *Twilight* books or movies and/or had read or seen every entry in the *True Blood* series. They even dressed like vampires, pale-skinned, black clothing, red lips. In discussion, I'd come to see, they always asked questions that were slightly too specific, like, "How would a vampire know it's dark enough to rise?" and "Where in Slovakia would I find a vampire today?" Even though I made sure to mention in every single class that vampires weren't real, this news never seemed to sink in. They were creepy.

The fourth group are the vast majority of any class, the I'm Heres. They're here. In class. They will do most of the work. They will occasionally be interested, but mostly not. They'll get it done, though. They're there.

And the fifth and final group were arrayed between the True Believers and I'm Heres: the Working Something Outs. They were in the class because it was an interesting and (word on the street correctly said) relatively easy way to fulfill a requirement, but also because they, too, were scaredy-cats. Like me, they were trying to find a balance between fascination and fear. Several of them asked questions about trigger warnings, which had never been an issue in my writing classes. Lost on what to say, exactly, about the trigger warnings for a course about vampires—the course title being one—I invited them to stop by to discuss with me after class.

Among the several students who did—Try Hards who wanted to be sure I knew their name, and True Believers who wanted me to know that they wrote *Twilight* fan fiction, since they assumed, wildly incorrectly, that I really liked vampires, too—was a young woman from the Working Something Outs. I'll call her Eva.

Eva said, "I just wanted to let you know about my triggers."

"Okay," I said. "Great."

"So I'm scared of blood. And gore. And… vampires."

There was a silence as I tried to think of how I could reiterate that the course *Vampire! Blood and Empire!* had an awful lot of blood and vampires in it.

"Well," I finally said, "it's going to be tricky."

"Yeah. I'm just trying to work some stuff out," she said, almost apologetically. A light bulb went off for me. This young woman was a scaredy-cat, just like me. Fascinated and terrified, in equal measure.

"I got you," I said. "Kind of like aversion therapy?" I said. She nodded.

"Okay," I said. "Let's see how it goes."

I thought Eva was brave. And her bravery made me more courageous. I started looking at the stack of vampire-themed literature I had to read for the class, and instead of finding an excuse in my scaredy-cat-ness not to do it, I wanted to be prepared for Eva's sake, to be able to tell her and, for that matter, the rest of the class but especially the Working Something Outs, what was genuinely terrifying and what was merely intriguing. Of course, that's personal, but we humans do tend to find the same things scary, so I thought I could help.

When Eva came back a couple of classes later, she wanted to know if I had any advice on how to read horror without completely freaking herself out, a very reasonable question. I answered without hesitation, as I had developed some tricks from my reading for the class.

"Lights on," I said. "Before 8:00 p.m. Eat a snack. Take notes. Make sure there are other people around."

She nodded, resolute, and, I assume, set off for the nearest Starbucks to read the literature for the course.

Skipping the Starbucks I, too, turned my living room lights up brightly and put an Office Noises playlist on, while I made my way through Bram Stoker's *Dracula*, Sheridan Le Fanu's *Carmilla*, and Anne Rice's *Interview with the Vampire*. I quickly realized that I was no longer a seven-year-old terrified by cheesy old photographs. It's not that the books were power-less over me as an adult. Stoker created an uncanny valley of a main character, creeping all over Europe on his quest for fresh victims. Le Fanu managed to write an engagingly pas-sionate relationship between young women that unfortunately involves blood-sucking. And Rice's portrayal of century after century of Southern history and the opportunities for brutal-ity offered within each era is uncomfortably familiar for the American reader.

And yet, each book is flawed, which I could only see after years of studying literature, learning about writing, and read-ing so many books. Stoker doesn't seem to have ever used one word when twenty will do, and the book's epistolary struc-ture is innately distancing.[111] *Carmilla* does not, I am sorry to say, make a ton of logical sense. And Rice also seems at times to have been paid by the word, perhaps slightly more per adjective.

When I pointed out (or allowed the students to draw out) these mild criticisms of the writing, the response was mostly predictable: the True Believers ignored anything that wasn't proof of vampires living among us. The Try Hards wrote down what I said and nodded in agreement. The I'm Heres were there. But the Working Something Outs, they were

---

111   How scared do you want me to be for you if you had the time to write and post this letter?

riveted. The idea that they could have some control over the warring factions inside of them, that some peace might be found between their fascination with scary things and their fear of the same things, was extremely welcome. I heard them sharing my laughably basic reading tips as if they were gospel, and wondered if the campus Starbucks's employees had noticed how many of their patrons appeared to be reading *Dracula*. And so, we made our way through the semester, slowly but without incident.

I kept an eye on Eva, especially when we watched—again, this was not my syllabus; I do what I'm told—Francis Ford Coppola's *Bram Stoker's Dracula*. (Yes, in case you're wondering, I did present it as Shannon Reed's Francis Ford Coppola's *Bram Stoker's Dracula*, which was only improved by a student who referred to it as *Ruth's Chris's Steak House's Dracula* in a paper.) That movie caused me to backslide; unlike a book, which I could adeptly pick apart, I knew a movie could wreak havoc on my psyche, so much so that I ultimately wimped out on watching it at home and instead viewed it for the first time with the class. I kept an eye on Eva while I did, especially when blood started spurting. She looked a little pale, which I could tell because I kept the lights on and encouraged them to take notes, to the groans of disappointment from the True Believers.

As we approached the blood-and-gore-swamped climax, with Gary Oldman chewing away on all available scenery and not a few extras, I felt a little queasily scared myself. This movie was a lot, for sure. Oldman's performance was like the Universal Studios books on acid. What if I started to break

WHY WE READ279

down, the equivalent of yelling for my mom, but this time in front of one hundred and fifty undergraduates?

Out of the corner of my eye, I saw Eva slump down in her seat and look to me, a clear sign that she was triggered. I scurried up the aisle next to her.

"Hey," I said, "you can step outside if you need to. But it's just a movie."

She frowned, torn.

I continued, "And the movie is based on a book that's just a bunch of letters."

She started to smile. "And numbers," she said.

That was not the kind of letters I meant, and I suppose I could have corrected her, but you know what? She was not wrong.

"Right," I whispered back. "You can—we can do this."

She took a deep breath and picked up her pencil, writing, *Dracula attacks people* in large letters in her notebook, while I sat down in the aisle next to her seat (almost blocking the view of an I'm Here who was… there). She made it through that class, and she made it through the course. I don't know if the aversion therapy fixed her, but she left happier than the day she arrived.

The truth is, I didn't like *Bram Stoker's Dracula*. I didn't like any of the books I taught in that class, either, even the ones that surprised me—I mean, who even knew that there was a nineteenth-century lesbian-ish vampire novel? But horror is not my jam. I'm glad, though, that horror doesn't have the same power over me, anymore. I know, I know, the authors wanted me to be scared. I'm circumventing their aim. But I genuinely believe that while we might be interested to know what an author intended with their work, our response to it comes from our own unique selves. If I want to make a list of the ways Stephen King deploys the color red in *It*, instead of being entirely terrified by *It*, that is my business.

Oh, please. As if I could never read *It*.

By the way, one of the True Believers gave me a copy of some fan fiction they wrote, inspired by the class, they said. When I started to read it, I quickly realized that it was about a professor who taught a class on vampires but who actually was a vampire. I was fascinated. I was terrified. I didn't finish reading it.

TO LEARN HOW TO DIE
(AND HOW TO LIVE)

I grew up in a mortality-aware household. The concept of death is one I don't remember learning; it was always there, something I understood as best as I could without personal experience. My father was a Lutheran pastor, and his work suffused our lives, with its proximity to life and death, sickness and health. In the same way that I imagine other families heard about difficult customers at the store and the tiring demands of office work, my dad told us about trips to the hospital to comfort the dying and visits at the funeral home to plan a service (but also hang out with the guys who worked there). The phone rang in the middle of the night to call him to the hospice a few miles up the road. A news story about a car crash could send him scrambling to reach a parishioner who had been affected. Mortality was just always there.

And while he was always respectful to the ill, the dying and dead, and their families, Dad never failed to share with us the strange humanity that popped up in hospitals and funeral homes:

the guy in the hospital after a heart attack who insisted that his family bring him a bucket of fried chicken; the man who ordered that Charlie Daniels's recording of "The Devil Went Down to Georgia" play as his casket was recessed (the family complied); the woman who chose to wear a full on Mafia-wife outfit to her brother's funeral (including a hat with a veil); the moment a funeral-home worker almost knocked over a lit candle at the front of the sanctuary, nearly setting a spray of roses on fire.

Most of my understanding of mortality was in this vein, actually: more concerned with the living, and their foibles, than the dead. But still, I was never unaware of mortality. When I chose *Carpe diem* as my personal motto (appearing underneath my senior picture in my high-school yearbook, so you know I meant it), it wasn't entirely flippant. People in my dad's church had died at fourteen, nineteen, twenty-five, thirty, thirty-seven, and so on, and I had heard about their lives and their deaths. I knew everyone only had so much time. In a strange way, I found it comforting.

But in all of this, what I never understood was the fact of my own upcoming death. I didn't think of my own mortality, only others'. I suspect we humans are programmed to believe ourselves immortal, but given my upbringing I really was unusually unaware of my fragility, a von Trapp who has never wondered if they could sing.

Reading *Being Mortal: Medicine and What Matters in the End*, a 2014 nonfiction bestseller by the writer and doctor Atul Gawande, changed all of that for me. Eventually.

Being Mortal contains many threads of remarkable writing. Gawande begins with an indictment of modern medicine and "how often [it] fails the people it is supposed to help" by always prioritizing any kind of life over *quality* of life. The story Gawande tells of his patient, Sarah, who lost opportunities to close out her life meaningfully because she was always urged—including by him—to fight the incurable cancer that would eventually kill her, is particularly haunting.

The book is also a rich series of anecdotes and explorations of how we age in America: what we do right, and what we do wrong, and how the process has changed over the last century, becoming more institutionalized (we used to mostly die at home), more independent (we used to age and die around family), and lonelier. Tying those threads together, Gawande writes about his own father's decline and eventual death, allowing readers into a life well-lived, full and rich to the end, and demonstrating that this was so because of his father's willingness to consider his own mortality. Gawande writes evocatively about the question that emerges from these considerations: "If independence is what we live for, what do we do when it can no longer be sustained?"

Answering that question, or at least exploring possible answers, is the book's purpose. What I most think of, though, when considering *Being Mortal*, is the series of tidy little sentence bombs Gawande tosses every once in a while, neatly designed to remind readers that the considerations he brings up are not just about our aging parents. We, too, will die. Here are a few:

"Although the [aging] processes can be slowed…they cannot be stopped."

"Decline remains our fate; death will someday come."

"Death is the enemy. But the enemy has superior forces.
Eventually, it wins."

You will note that the above sentences are highly inclusive
of the reader (and the writer, too). It's rare to find a book in
the first person plural that is so adamant and assured that everyone reading it is definitely included in the *we*. And yet,
bolstered by that inherent belief that everyone else was mortal but not me, I did not apply any of this to myself the first
time I read it. Instead, I thought about my dad.

2015 was an *annus horribilis* for my family: the year we lost
my father. It's inevitably a year crosshatched with grief for
me, my brother and sister-in-law, my dad's sisters and their
spouses, his friends, and, most of all, my mom. Dad had gradually become ill for many years—diabetes, heart issues, other
problems—and in January of that year, he was diagnosed with
liver cancer. As the year wound on, he grew sicker and sicker
and then eventually so ill that he knew he was dying, which
in September, he did, reasonably at peace, shunning most of
the technically life-prolonging but not life-enhancing medical interventions Gawande rails against. Having seen what
they did to his parishioners, Dad had long said he would re-
ject them, and in the end, he stuck to his vow.
    Gawande writes about this kind of aging in *Being Mortal*,
which I coincidentally first read in early 2015. In the past, he
notes, aging was an abrupt decline: "Life and health would
putter along nicely... Then illness would hit and the bottom

would drop out…" But because of our superior health care these days, our descent into decline looks less like a cliff and "more like a hilly road down a mountain." This precisely captured my father's experience, so I was immediately engaged by Gawande's book, moreover when he wrote, "we may not be able to stave off the damage, but we can stave off death." Exactly, I thought, remembering my father's ever-worsening symptoms and ever-more frequent trips to the ER. I read the entire book in a matter of days, even while completing my MFA, teaching and frequently driving ninety minutes to visit my parents. It was that compelling.

After finishing it, I thought constantly of Gawande's book, especially his exploration of what would constitute an acceptable level of living to be worth staying alive for, particularly of the professor emeritus who tells his adult daughter he's willing to stay alive if he can eat chocolate ice cream and watch football on TV. Prompted by *Being Mortal*, I was wondering what would constitute an acceptable level of living for my father and when I might need to step up to help him articulate that and protect it for him.

Now, as it turned out, my father made his own decisions until the end, with my mother's support, so my brother and I were barely involved in what he chose. But I was still glad to have been given the chance to think about such things. Gawande is adept at depicting the confusion of aging and dying, particularly in how we're conditioned to believe that to be ill, to be dying, is somehow a failure (even though, as he relentlessly notes, we all will experience illness and death), which was comforting.

For someone like me, a how-many-rows-from-the-air-plane-exit counter, the scariest part of my father's dying might have been that I had no idea at all what would happen. I don't mean the afterlife—I was pretty sure about what my father believed—but the actuality of the process. After all, Dad was the person who knew the most about dying in our family, and he was busy, well, dying. I had to look to an outside source, and *Being Mortal*, with its willingness to talk about uncomfortable truths, was it. Along with my faith and the way I was raised, it allowed me to make choices that were not solely the result of anxiety and panic, which meant that for at least half of the time, I behaved lovingly during those terrible and wonderful weeks.

In my second read of *Being Mortal*, undertaken specifically to write this essay, I had a rougher time. Don't get me wrong—the book remains beautifully written and deeply affecting. I cried at Sarah's story, again, and found every anecdote about an adult child talking with a parent about their end-of-life decisions powerful. These stories hit home anew: my father had my mother to rely on, but if everything goes well, Justin and I will be who my mother turns to when, as Gawande writes, "[a]s a person's end draws near, there comes a moment when responsibility shifts to someone else to decide what to do." I believe that this moment is many years, decades, away, but still.

But really, the roughness is because I no longer see mortality as everyone else's problem. I have aged (from forty-one when my father died to forty-eight as I write this), I have lived through a pandemic, I have new, less easily understood health issues, and I recognize that many of my friends have lost some or all of the generations between them and death. I understand that if I am lucky enough that the friends of my youth become the friends of my golden years, we will need to discuss such things. Gawande's meditations are not for far-off, future me, but for me now.

I've read very few horror stories in my life, but when I did, if they were any good, or if I was of sufficiently persuadable mood, there was always a moment in which my surroundings began to take on the qualities of the book—if it was cold, wasn't I cold, too? If it was filled with menace, wasn't my living room menace-filled, too? The spell was broken by altering either my environment (heat on! music on!) or my reading (book put away!). As I read *Being Mortal*, something similar happened to me, as I felt weighed down by the grim future I sensed for myself. I felt a real sadness, and real fear, about the inevitable decline that Gawande foresaw. I honestly don't think I'd ever really understood the truth before, that I was going to die, in some specific way, at some specific point in the future. I had to walk away from the book, turn on lights, turn on the TV, and find some high-quality chocolate to eat. Someone else's mortality, even that of a person you dearly love, is one thing; the realization of your own is a different beast entirely. I cannot ever shake that sadness.

And yet, several weeks on, having finished *Being Mortal* again, I'm ultimately glad I reread it. The book is far too complex and clear-eyed to boil down to one aphorism. In fact, to be fair, I don't think it really has aphorisms at all. But I'm left thinking about one sentence in particular: "Our ultimate goal, after all, is not a good death but a good life to the very end." I trust Gawande's wisdom, as he has seen so many lives and so many deaths, and I'm grateful that he found the time, somehow, to share these experiences in his book.

And so I find myself more appreciative of the beauty of my one precious life, as the poet Mary Oliver put it, of time with my mom and brother and sister-in-law and aunts and uncle. Of laughing with my students, debating the merits of television shows for hours with Andrew, of sewing and cooking and gardening. Visits to far-off friends, epic board game tournaments, trips to the theater, silly messages with my colleagues, hot cups of tea, brownies, and a friend to share both with. I find more pleasure in my reading, aware that perhaps there will be a time when I cannot lift a book, or read the words, or hear the recording. I find myself more aware of the goodness of my life, my face gently turned toward the bright but fading sun of being mortal.

BECAUSE ONCE MORE
WAS ENOUGH

I had difficulty figuring out what to *do* after my father had passed away, after the long descent of his final illness and the sharp, cold crack of his leaving. At first, as is so often the case, our schedule was completely filled. There was planning for the funeral, the viewing, the service itself, and the burial, and the day after—the first day of the rest of our lives, that is. There were cards and gifts to acknowledge, and people to look after, and being looked after myself, of course. There was a very large amount of food for my very small family, including a giant hubcap-size platter of finger sandwiches which I ate by the half dozen. Then there was saying goodbye to everyone who had traveled in, and one last night in my mom's house, and then, finally, when returning to teaching could be put off no longer, there was the sudden solitude of driving home alone, made worse by knowing I had left my mother in an otherwise-empty house.

Then everything got quiet, for the long period when active and bitterly painful grief intermingled with my daily life,

when I couldn't figure out how to spend my time. I carried
on teaching, I made my bed and meals, and I returned emails
and wrote, building my burgeoning career as a newly minted
MFA-holder who was turning out to be, of all things, a hu-
morist. I was glad to hear from just about anyone, even an editor rejecting my work with a form letter. Anything to settle
my mind in the looming quiet, potholed as I was with grief.

I just couldn't figure out what I could do during any moment not consumed by work, how I could avoid the waves of
grief always on their way into the shore. My father loved music
and had been interested in what I listened to as well, so unless
I wanted to weep continuously, no music could be played. I
watched television, but almost all of it seemed trite, or when
it wasn't, it hit too close to home. Movies were the same.

My one true love, books, were unexpectedly perilous. They
were of more comfort, but I couldn't quite figure out what to
read. At that time, everyone was talking about Helen Macdonald's *H Is for Hawk*, and it sounded like a wonderful book,
but it's about her father and his death, so I couldn't even crack
open either of the two copies I was given.[112] My comfort re-
reads were either too facile or hewed too close to my pain
(somehow, *Pride and Prejudice* seemed to do both, a light romance that happens to include an intense father/daughter
bond in Mr. Bennet and Lizzy), and because I had shared a
devotion to the United Kingdom with my dad, not even a
cozy book about the Queen solving crimes could save me.

I really longed to lose myself in a good book, in the most
necessary way—I was very tired of my weepy, grief-ridden,

112   I still have not. I'll consider it a sign of significant healing when I finally
      read it. Maybe after the tenth anniversary of his death.

exhausted self and wanted very, very much to be free of her, even for a bit—so I kept trying. Although I don't think there's yet been another period in my life when I was so quick to abandon a book after only a page or two—even spotting the word *Dad* could make me toss it aside, and it turns out that there are a lot of *Dad*s in a lot of books—I did finally find a solution: the *Harry Potter* series on audiobook.

I started with the first because it was familiar, available at the library, and my favorite of the series. I almost never listen to audiobooks—nothing against them, just not my jam—but that semester, I was teaching at a small university about a forty-five-minute drive from my home, which meant that I had to fill at least ninety minutes with something other than my own thoughts and memories and regrets. Say what you will about the *Harry Potter* books, flawed and faintly misogynistic as they may be, what they surely are is many pages long. Say, too, what you will about the audiobook-narrator Jim Dale's choice to voice all women as tremulously high-pitched, but he catches, and holds, your ear. Harry's loneliness as abjectly parentless spoke to me but told my truth slant enough that I could mostly listen without incident.[113] After a few weeks, I had finished the first book, and moved immediately on to the second, and concluded the entire set about halfway through the spring semester.

We are rightly aghast at the many horrible things J. K. Rowling has said or tweeted, and I don't want to defend her. I could not, in fact; we do not agree. Years before her recent horrors, though, what struck me in her books was the real

---

113   I did have to pull over several times when bad things happened to the Weasleys. On some level, I think my ancestors were Weasleys.

understanding of grief she showed through her characters. Harry, as my mom pointed out, is an abused and abandoned child, desperately mourning his parents, then Dumbledore. Snape has shaped his life around the gaping hole that is the loss of Lily. Ron grieves for his brother, Hermione for Cedric Diggory. Every actual adult in the books seems to be weighted down with some loss. As strange as it sounds to say about a book filled with magic and the highest-possible stakes, what kept me listening was the sense that the world of the books was filled with people longing for what they would never have again, not in this life, who could not magic away their deep regret. Nor could I.

I won't listen to the *Harry Potter* books again, I don't think. Too problematic and now too evocative of long, sad drives across northwestern Pennsylvania, where I kept track of how the leaves were dying and dead and I waited to feel better. But I'm glad I had them at that time.

TO TRY AGAIN

My colleague Jeff and I have a running joke that I will never, ever teach a poetry class at Pitt. By *running joke*, I really mean that every so often, when it appears that Jeff is trying to come up with someone who can take over an Introduction to Writing Poetry class, I shrilly assert that, ha ha ha, I definitely cannot ever do that, and Jeff, a gifted poet himself, patiently nods. He knows: I will do anything for love/Pitt, but I won't do that. You'll recollect that I've willingly taught a class on vampires, a subject that I both knew nothing about and was afraid of, so I hope it's clear just how scared I am of poetry.

Occasionally, a student will admit in their semester-end evaluation that what they learned in my writing class is that they're more of a reader than a writer.[114] Only in the world of poetry do I relate. In no other form of literature do I feel least like a writer and most like a reader.

There's a comfort in that, actually. I once asked Andrew,

---

114   And honestly, *good for them*. That is a great realization!

who is a deeply talented musical-theater performer—we met at a theater-training program in college—whether he was able to attend a musical performance without a pang of envy. "Not really," he said. "There's always a small part of me that thinks about the choices I would have made or whether I would have been as good as, or better than, the guy onstage."

I, tone-deaf and of minimal dance skill, do not attend musicals with this pang. I sit there, bedazzled to the point of tears, because I have no skin in the game. I read fiction and nonfiction, humor and scripts, the way Andrew watches a musical—with a tinge of jealousy and a healthy sense of eval-uation—but I read poetry the way I watch a musical: wow, I cannot do that, but good for you!

I know that there are no end to guides on how to read and understand poetry out there, and if they speak to you, fantas-tic. I've tried many of them. My brain starts to short-circuit after meter is mentioned; that is apparently the syllabic hill upon which my mind will die. I don't understand the forms or structure, the literary elements, the rhythm. Even rhyme schemes leave me perplexed. All I can really do is read poems and try to get out of them what I can.

And yet, I do *like* poetry. It's the genre I find most potently emotional. A poem I love can haunt me, the lines rolling over and over in my mind as I try to decide what they mean or, more to the point, what they mean to me. I think about the poems I love—W. S. Merwin's "Thanks," Elizabeth Bishop's "Casabianca," Kaylin Haught's "God Says Yes to Me"—more than I think about the stories or books I love. I once heard someone call poetry a heartbeat, and that sounds about right to me. You live with it, and sometimes, in moments of high emotion, you're very aware it's there.

In my own way, I've tried to understand and enjoy poetry, hesitantly at first, and then more valiantly over the last decade since I've been teaching writing. And I've developed a method, which you might enjoy trying, too, if poetry is something you'd like to appreciate more.

Reading about one poem a day is what works for me. Perhaps two. Any more than that, and the reading turns remedial, a corrective that feels like an assignment. But I can, and do, read one poem a day. I read it slowly, and I think about it, and then I put the book down, part of my morning devotions.

I started reading a poem a day in the late '90s. At the time, I was working on a master's at NYU, the campus of which is just a few blocks away from the famous Strand Book Store. I loved to kill time at that place, although I almost never bought anything, given my measly grad-student budget. On this particular day, I ended up browsing the poetry collections and picked up a book called *A Year in Poetry: A Treasury of Classic and Modern Verses for Every Date on the Calendar*, edited by Thomas E. Foster and Elizabeth C. Guthrie, published in 1995 (making it only a few years old at the time). Well, I thought, looking at the extremely 1990s woodcuts decorating the cover, even I can read a poem a day! I love all of my daily little rituals—Andrew says my production company should be called Creature of Habit Media—and adding another sounded good to me. So I bought the book and brought it home, leaving it on my bedside table to be rediscovered the next morning, when I read the poem for that date. I don't recall if I liked it, but I suspect I didn't, especially. But never mind, tomorrow was another day. I read the next poem the next day, and the next, and the next, and when the year ended, I flipped back to the beginning to do it again. And I've continued doing so for twenty years.

At first, I read too quickly, understood little, and was annoyed with poetry's opacity. I only liked the poems that told clear stories in modern English.[115] My favorite was John Mole's "The Impertinence of the Thing," recounting a meeting gone wrong between James Joyce and W. B. Yeats on the latter's fortieth birthday,[116] which wonderfully ends with the poet's realization that he is older now than both the greats, and can laugh with each one, and then all of them together.

Every other poem I liked was equally narrative and usually about someone famous. But through the years, I have expanded my interests. I read poetry more slowly. To be fair, I have more time to read, now, as well. And as I've lived with the book, I have grown fond of its offerings. I still would be very hard-pressed to tell you the form any particular poem takes (except, perhaps, for the one haiku…) and I cannot speak to the meter of any. Those qualities matter; as a creative-writing teacher, I value the forms, traditions, and patterns of writing and am embarrassed I do not know more about poetry. And yet, these poems have affected me all the same, illuminating how I see the world around me.

Some of my days or dates are now irrevocably intertwined with a poem. April 18 brings Henry Wadsworth Longfellow's propulsive (if historically suspect) "Paul Revere's Ride," and August 16, "The Battle of Bennington" by William Cul-

---

115   *Clear Poems in Modern English* is a book I would definitely buy.

116   Joyce told him, "You are too old for me to help."

len Bryant (with the haunting line "our blood shall steep the
ground we tread"). December 12 reminds me of Sir Toby's
thwarted attempt to sing a folk song set on that date in Shakespeare's *Twelfth Night* (the editors include the text of the song),
and Joyce Carol Oates's "An American Tradition" arrives on
Boxing Day to celebrate, as the first line says, "Returning gifts!"
an old tradition now mostly vanished in America, I think. As
someone who loathes Valentine's Day, I turn with joy to Peter
Reading's "15th February," a "love" poem gone very wrong.

After so many years of living with this book's poems, I look
forward to its reminders of the more obscure holidays, of reading about the "season of mists and mellow fruitfulness" in John
Keats's "To Autumn" around the beginning of the season (September 19), and celebrating St. Crispin's Day on October 25,
with Shakespeare's King Henry V's "we few, we happy few"
speech from the play of the same name. On April 14, I mark
Abraham Lincoln's last day alive with the book's excerpt from
Stephen Vincent Benét's very long poem about the president. It's
no longer especially well-known but, like all of the poems in the
book, feels very popular to me, so I'm always surprised that no
one really knows what I'm talking about when I bring it up.[117]

And then there are the holidays that don't exist at all, except for me. I privately celebrate when I work my way around
to my favorites: Alice Fulton's "Another Troy" (on March
16, about the fall of a bridge in upstate New York that managed not to kill anyone),[118] Paul Goodman's "Don Larsen's

---

117   This inadvertently creates the impression that I am someone who reads a
      lot of poetry, which I am publicly disavowing.

118   I mentioned this poem to someone after a bridge fell (and also did not
      kill) in Pittsburgh, and they were very impressed by the depth of my
      literary knowledge. Again: not true!

Perfect Game," recounting the only perfect game pitched in a World Series, on October 8, and Bret Harte's "What the Engines Said" for the May 10 anniversary of the opening of the Pacific Railroad.

Not every poem entices me. I love Grace Paley, but the gloomy poem of hers, which is unfortunately my birthday's poem, brings me down every time. It begins with a beguiling portrait of the Native peoples of what is now New York State, and ends with their death from smallpox. Not very cheerful. To be fair, I think that was Paley's intention.

In general, the editors favored white men too much, and especially white men of the 1500 and 1600s; I skip most of the Renaissance-era play excerpts every year. I don't read the several pieces in Middle English, either, a language I don't understand, and which actually isn't close enough to our English to figure out, you guys, come on.

But lately, I've been challenging myself to read the poems I heretofore skipped, a choice almost always made (when not for Middle-English-y reasons) because the poems were Too Long, a designation I give to any longer than, oh, twelve lines. This is both silly and lazy, so I've been trying harder. I'm not always successful; Hart Crane is not my guy. But I loved Richard Katrovas's "Kings' Day, 1984" when I finally settled down to read it. It concludes:

Tonight,
The cathedrals of Europe are cocked
And ready; the apartment is clean and quiet.
One nervous fool twitching in the dark,
I burn with hope like a star.

And thus I make my way through poetry, picking and choosing, inept and easily dissuaded but at least still trying. This collection encouraged me to read more and to buy other collections, so now I often read a poem from another source as well as my poem a day. My choices are neither sophisticated nor hip, I'm afraid; I've read Billy Collins, W. S. Merwin, Mary Oliver, and poetry collections themed around Ireland, New York and—currently—American religion. More often than not, I don't especially feel a kinship to the poem I've read (although, when I do, it's a magical and lovely thing). Obviously, my aversion to poems that are Too Long, my lack of knowledge about how poetry works, and my fondness for narrative all work against much improvement in my breadth of poetry appreciation.

Clearly, Jeff should definitely not schedule me to teach a poetry class. But I'm grateful to my decades-long poetry-immersion project. It turns out that living with a little poetry every day lured me into liking poems, or even loving them. I have become that fool for poetry, twitching, burning with hope, like a star.

TO MOTIVATE US

Have you read the modern-day classic, *Too Much Mime on My Hands*? It's a guidebook to/memoir about learning how to be a mime, just in case the title didn't immediately jog your memory. Or perhaps you've read *Antiquities and Me*, another memoir, this time by a midlevel Manhattan-based antiques dealer? If not those, how about *Potatoes and More: My Farmer's Life*, which I doubt needs any further explanation, except to say that the *and More* was cauliflower.

So look, I already know that it's highly unlikely you've read any of these books, unless you're the grandchild of Mr. Antiquities or Mr. Farmer—I sincerely doubt even his family read Mr. Mime's book. Also, to be fair, I've slightly changed the titles. Anyways, I've read all of them, and they were all terrible. The mime book was punishingly verbose, taking perhaps four hundred pages to tell the story of mime. Mime! The antiquities guy missed no opportunities to settle scores—low-stakes, extremely petty scores—with his family and former colleagues, including a chapter devoted to how his ex–business partner didn't know how to polish brass. And the farmer, well, he seemed sweet, but he didn't really have a lyrical instinct for writing about the passing of the seasons. There were a lot of sentences like, "Every harvest season, when the potatoes were ready to harvest, we harvested them."

I read each of these books because I was assigned to do so; not, thankfully, by an educational institution but by the publishing company I worked for in the case of Mr. Mime and by the publishing website I wrote reviews for in my twenties and thirties for the other two. Mr. Mime's was a manuscript, and it's possible that if someone had decided to take a chance on it (which my employer most definitely did not), it would have been winnowed by about two hundred pages to be a perfectly good guide for the three people in the world who want to become professional mimes. The other two, the ones that existed as books already, were self-published, likely without the benefit of a professional editor. I'm not against self-publishing, but in my limited experience, self-published books suffer, as these did, from the lack of editorial input. Perhaps an experienced editor could have urged Mr. Antiquities away from the brass-polishing and into more depth about his actual understanding of old things. Alas.

I should note that I've read plenty of terrible books published by major publishing companies, too, ones that have had not just the benefit of an editor but also, I suspect, the ministrations of a ghost writer as well as a support team of designers, copy editors, and publicists. The very worst of these, I'm so sorry to say, was by Shirley MacLaine, the actor/singer/dancer who wrote a series of books in the 1980s and '90s about her spiritual beliefs. Said beliefs were—I'm using a technical term here—*woo-woo*, so the books were already a lot. But this one in particular was called *Out on a Leash*, and it was about her dog Terry's[119] spiritual beliefs and death. In it, she directly addresses the reader in ways such as, "Terry and I have been talking..." which added an element of actual insanity to the woo-woo-ness. I truly apologize if you have lost a dog and found this book meaningful, and I also apologize to Shirley MacLaine, a great talent who honestly deserves better than the best-sellers which she supposedly wrote. But it was a terrible book.

Another that stands out for me is *The Day I Shot Cupid*, which is by the actor Jennifer Love Hewitt, about her love life. I highly doubt Hewitt wrote any of this god-awful book—at least I hope not, since the portion I remember was her advice that we should bedazzle our vaginas, and I really want that to have been entirely made-up. I was so distraught about how awful this advice was that a friend who also worked in publishing explained that no one was actually going to buy Hewitt's book—the entire point was the publicity that the house generated by publishing it. Perhaps. It's still available on Amazon, though. Please do not bedazzle your groins.

For all that I loathed reading these books—and I should note that, especially at a younger age, before reading my students' work in front of them had taught me to keep a better poker face, I was an aggressively emotive reader, sighing, slumping, groaning, rolling my eyes, sighing some more—I am ultimately grateful that I did. At some point in the over five hundred books I read to review, my perception of books, or at least of books that were currently being released,

---

119   Yes, Terry was a terrier.

changed. I stopped thinking of writing and publishing a book as something very few (white, male, rich) people got to do and started thinking of publishing as something that Shirley MacLaine's dog's ghostwriter got to do.

I'm being facetious, of course. It's true that it's hard to publish a book. Terry the Dog only got to because he belonged to a very famous person. But the broad point is also roughly true: books get published because the writing is good but also because of luck, fame, and whim. An okay book about a zeitgeist-y topic is more likely to get published than an excellent book on a trend that has passed. An obvious, targetable market for a book increases the likelihood that a publisher will take it on. That's capitalism, baby, and actually quite freeing to realize.

Don't get me wrong—I care about the craft of writing, and I want to write well myself... and as a reader, I definitely prefer books that are well-written. But that's not only (always? often?) what gets published.

In the end, I found those terrible books incredibly motivating. I thought, If those authors could publish a book, who's to say I can't? I thought, At least I can write better than that! I thought, I have more to say than Mr. Antiquities! I thought, I have more to talk about than potatoes!

Wanting to share the contents of your soul is a great reason to be a writer, but I've found pretty consistently that being a petty, envious wretch is also motivating. It made me so angry that Shirley MacLaine's dog had a book and I did not. It motivated me.

And, since you're holding this book, you know that it worked.

TO MAKE US CRY (II)

I'm a crier by nature, as I've shared, but as I've aged, my reasons for tearing up have become more elusive, even to me. Where once I could predict a crying spell, like spotting an East Texas thunderstorm moving across the landscape, now they arrive fast and sharp, like hail in New England on a March day. More and more frequently, I find myself wiping away tears while asking with plaintive frustration, "Wait, why am I crying right now?"

I had one of those spells this morning while holding a very old book in the rare-books room of the Health Sciences Library at the University of Pittsburgh. Our group of visiting scholars had been warned not to lick or cough or sneeze on the old books, a warning that I had impressed on my soul, as I do with all advice from librarians. Thus, the arrival of unexpected tears—one moment I was paging carefully through the book, scanning, not terribly attentive, the next I was sobbing—mostly triggered my consternation at producing forbidden fluid.

I didn't know I was going to cry! I wanted to yell, as I grabbed a tissue from the librarian's desk, keeping my face averted from anything old. *I did not deliberately get bodily fluids on your books!*

Of course, no one was paying me the least bit of attention, intent as they all were on their own research in their own old books. The librarian didn't notice me, either, thankfully, as she passed around cloth gloves to scholars who wanted to touch very, very old books. So I wiped away my tears, resanitized my hands, and went back to the book I had been looking at to figure out what had made me cry.

It was a dead and delicate weight in my hands, slightly larger than a brick, the leather cover somewhere between *pliable* and *about to crack into dust at any moment*. The brown leather could have been cow or ostrich or human, for all I knew. It was stained by bodily fluids dating back to the French Revolution. I opened it again, holding it away from me.

I turned back to its title page: *The Anatomy of the Human Body*, written by William J. Cheselden and it was the 7th edition published in 1750. I don't work in the health-sciences field and am not a scholar of the body or of medical texts. I have a body, but most days—although perhaps it ought—that fact does not move me to tears.

I vaguely remember a signature across the title page. I find handwriting moving, especially dashed-off handwriting from two hundred years ago. Was that the trigger? I turned to the opening pages to see the original owner's loopy signature: Finlay Miller. I felt gratitude that Finlay had taken good enough care of his book that it could be passed down, again and again, to end up in a beautiful room of old books at the school where I teach. But it wasn't a very strong gratitude, I

must say. It was more of an acknowledgment, the way Andrew says, "That's very cool," before changing the subject.

I moved on to the first pages of the book, looking for a
meaningful city of publication or a touching dedication. Since
my father's death, any author thanking their parent, even
perfunctorily at the end of the acknowledgments, can start
my tears, but I found nothing. Honestly, I was beginning to
worry. Had I transitioned from being a person who cries a
lot to a person who cries unexpectedly to a person who cries
for no reason at all?

I flipped another page and began to read a note from the
author to his readers: "This edition is a tenth part larger than
the former; not increased by description but by observations
upon the uses and mechanism of the parts, with operations
and cases in surgery."

My eyes prickled again, and I almost laughed. This ca-
joling note, urging readers to appreciate that the book was
one-tenth larger than the prior editions, is what had gotten
to me. I understood the need to entice readers to not just flip
through but actually buy your book. Authors are not just artists but also salespeople, trying to convince readers that our
products are pleasing, will help them learn, are worth their
while. That note of persistence in the face of what must have
seemed impossible—that somehow Cheselden could come
up with the words that would convince some random man
months in the future that he must indeed buy this book—
was deeply familiar to me. I just hadn't realized it was as old
as the book I was holding.

I've wheedled the same way. While I ought to have been
examining fascinating and rare books with my fellow schol-

ars, I spent hours worrying over the book I was beginning to piece together. I worried whether I would ever write a book that anyone would want to buy or publish or even read in my lifetime. What would I say in my query letters, my book proposal, my preface to get people to not just pick up but buy my book?

In Cheselden's note, from four hundred years ago, I see myself and the hustle of being a writer. "The plates are more in number, larger, better designed and better executed than those which were in the former editions," he wrote, "which has unavoidably enhanced the price of this [edition]." *It's worth more so it costs more*, he cries. *Please, please, buy this book!*

His hustle worked: Finlay Miller bought his book, and wrote his name in it. Likely, others did, too. But it was this one, this copy, that had made it through so many years of avoiding flood and plague and fire and book-burners, that had ended up in my negligent, tear-strewn hands. I had found a compatriot. I hoped this book was the eighteenth-century equivalent of a bestseller.

I closed the book gently and walked over to the librarian's desk and sanitized my hands again, just in case. As I did so, I watched my colleagues lift and turn pages, billing and cooing over the old volumes like a flock of pigeons. How we all love these books. I teared up again, but this time, I knew why.

BECAUSE WE ARE
WHAT WE READ

I know that the monster is at the end of the book, and he means no harm.

I know the Lorax speaks for the trees, and I should, too.

I know I ought to stay away from lollipops, and that sometimes there are terrible, horrible, no-good, very bad days, even in Australia.

I know that you can tie up a pig's bladder and use it as a balloon on butchering day, and that when a man drives several miles in his sled to deliver you home in a snowstorm, he likes you.

I know that kindred spirits are the best friends.

I know that writers hide out in garrets and eat apples and marry twinkly-eyed professors, if they can find one. (I haven't yet, but my hair *is* my one great beauty.)

I know that when you address God, you have to identify yourself as the speaker.

I know what happens to a raisin in the sun.

I know that once you give up your name, you can't have another, not in this life.

I know that we few, we happy few, are a band of brothers.

I know that you watch the rest of the world through a window... while you finish the hat.

I know that saints and poets maybe, well, they do some.

I know how to debone a chicken, although I never will, and that Stir-up Sunday is the day for making my Christmas pudding, although I never do. I know why eggs are called deviled, and what spices make it Coronation Chicken, and where one could get those spices (and an oyster knife) in Rego Park, Queens, if one wanted them. I know on which days you shouldn't buy the fish special. I know fifteen recipes for chocolate cake. If pressed, I can provide instructions on making an egg-and-mayonnaise aspic, which I do not recommend.

I know what it felt like to be in London in the Blitz.

I've cried with President Abraham Lincoln and plotted with Cool Girl Amy and brought the necklace home to Africa.

I know how old Paris is and how weird stone circles are and why you don't take your boots off in a snowstorm if they're soaked through.

I know that not all lotteries are good.

I know why we stop by woods on a snowy evening.

I have sung opera in a South American country just before being taken hostage.

I have hung out in Twyla Tharp's studio.

I survived the 1928 hurricane in the Everglades.

I know many, many details about David Bowie's 1984 *Serious Moonlight* tour.

I know why the caged bird sang.

I know where the Underground Railroad ran.

I know what John Brown said before he was hanged. I was there. John Wilkes Booth, too. I saw him fall.

I was at Columbine, I was in New Orleans, I was in Johnstown when the flood hit, I saw the plane go down into a field in Somerset County. I watched the plague destroy most everything in the 1600s. I saw the Mormons rip through the American West. I climbed Everest and didn't come back down. I saw my city silent and still in March of 2020.

I know all about Thursday Next, and Miss Marple, and Kinsey Millhone, and the Misfit.

I have watched so many people fall in love: with each other, with someone new, with the forbidden, with the obvious. Epiphanies, I've seen dozens. Realizations, hundreds more. Plot twists, I've been shocked, unconvinced, and skeptical. I have laughed, a lot, in space, in Bath, in the Pacific Northwest, backstage at *SNL,* with Steve Martin at Disneyland.

I have learned to macramé. I have fixed my toilet. I have identified poison ivy. I can sketch you a half-decent silhouette.

I've been to Pemberley, to Plum Creek, to the Orchard House,
to Buckingham Palace, more times than I can count. I've read
poems, and Bible verses, and stories, and articles, and song
lyrics, and books. So many, many books.

All of it, really, has been good, even the book about mimes.
Even Terry and Shirley. Even the whale-semen chapter. It
was all worth reading.

Without ever really experiencing any of it, I know it all.

Because books taught me.

★ ★ ★ ★ ★

LIST OF BOOKS
AND WORKS MENTIONED

A Wrinkle in Time by Madeleine L'Engle

Strega Nona by Tomie dePaola

The Wheels on the Bus by Anonymous

The Snowy Day by Ezra Jack Keats

Bel Canto by Ann Patchett

Little Women by Louisa May Alcott

Manual to a 1988 Chevrolet Corsica

The *Little House* series by Laura Ingalls Wilder

The *Anne of Green Gables* series by Lucy Maud Montgomery

The Wizard of Oz and subsequent Oz books by Frank L. Baum (esp. *The Patchwork Girl of Oz*)

The *Nancy Drew* series by Carolyn Keene

The *Harry Potter* series by J. K. Rowling

The *Goosebumps* series by R. L. Stine

The *Baby-sitters Club* series by Ann M. Martin

The *Sweet Valley High* series by Francine Pascal

Flowers in the Attic by V. C. Andrews

Chronicles of Narnia by C. S. Lewis

The Hunger Games by Suzanne Collins

The *Percy Jackson* series by Rick Riordan

The *Divergent* series by Veronica Roth

The *Game of Thrones* series by George R. R. Martin

The *Outlander* series by Diana Gabaldon

The *A Is for Alibi/Kinsey Millhone* series by Sue Grafton

The *Mitford* series by Jan Karon

The *Wolf Hall* series by Hilary Mantel

The *Dublin Murder Squad* series by Tana French

Multiple series by Alexander McCall Smith

Dear Fahrenheit 451 by Annie Spence

The Dig by John Preston

A random assortment of tourist brochures about ancient sites in the United Kingdom

Foundation: The History of England from Its Earliest Beginnings to the Tudors by Peter Ackroyd

How the Irish Saved Civilization by Thomas Cahill

Some book about the constellations for astronomy class

"The Highwayman" by Alfred Noyes

Tess of the D'Urbervilles by Thomas Hardy

"The Legend of Sleepy Hollow" by Washington Irving

Mrs. Dalloway by Virginia Woolf

The Crucible by Arthur Miller

The Grapes of Wrath by John Steinbeck

Little Fires Everywhere by Celeste Ng

Conversations with Friends by Sally Rooney

The Ocean at the End of the Lane by Neil Gaiman

The Great Gatsby by F. Scott Fitzgerald

Wuthering Heights by Emily Brontë

Dracula by Bram Stoker

Moby Dick by Herman Melville

A Tale of Two Cities by Charles Dickens

The Tragedy of Romeo and Juliet by William Shakespeare

Frankenstein, or A Modern Prometheus by Mary Shelley

Ethan Frome by Edith Wharton

I Know Why the Caged Bird Sings by Maya Angelou

Narrative of the Life of Frederick Douglass, American Slave by Frederick Douglass

Beowulf by Anonymous

Book Lovers by Emily Henry

Team of Rivals by Doris Kearns Goodwin

The Vanity Fair Diaries by Tina Brown

On Writing by Stephen King

A random Louis L'Amour paperback

Are You There God? It's Me, Margaret by Judy Blume

Ramona and Beezus by Beverly Cleary

Tinker, Tailor, Soldier, Spy by John le Carré

Modern Lovers by Emma Straub

Olive Kitteridge by Elizabeth Strout

The House at Pooh Corner by A. A. Milne

All That Glitters by Danielle Steele

"The Dead" by James Joyce

Pride and Prejudice by Jane Austen

Persuasion by Jane Austen

Old MacDonald Had a Farm by Anonymous

Pat the Bunny by Dorothy Kunhardt

Chicka Chicka Boom Boom by Bill Martin, Jr. and John Archambault

The Monster at the End of the Book by Jon Stone

Farmer Duck by Martin Waddell

The Westing Game by Ellen Raskin

The Mouse and the Motorcycle by Beverly Cleary

Howl by Allen Ginsberg

Where the Red Fern Grows by Wilson Rawls

Holidays on Ice by David Sedaris

The Fault in Our Stars by John Green

David Bowie's Serious Moonlight: The World Tour Book by Chet Flippo

Heart of Darkness by Joseph Conrad

The Diary of a Young Girl by Anne Frank

The Liars' Club by Mary Karr

The Bacchae by Euripides

The Namesake by Jhumpa Lahiri

The Interestings by Meg Wolitzer

The Catcher in the Rye by J. D. Salinger

My Brilliant Friend by Elena Ferrante

Their Eyes Were Watching God by Zora Neale Hurston

Gender Trouble by Judith Butler

The Decameron by Boccaccio

Don Quixote by Miguel de Cervantes

The Known World by Edward P. Jones

The Things They Carried by Tim O'Brien

Homegoing by Yaa Gyasi

The Tragedy of Hamlet, Prince of Denmark by William Shakespeare

Wonder by R. J. Palacio

Jane Eyre by Charlotte Brontë

A Separate Peace by John Knowles

The Tenant of Wildfell Hall by Anne Brontë

Mrs. Beeton's Book of Household Management by Isabella Beeton

The Moosewood Cookbook by Mollie Katzen

Seriously Delish: 150 Recipes for People Who Totally Love Food by Jessica Merchant

The Short Stack Cookbook: Ingredients That Speak Volumes by Nick Fauchald and Kaitlyn Goalen

300 Ways to Serve Eggs by Anonymous

Salt Fat Acid Heat by Samin Nosrat

Best of Amish Cooking by a (presumably Amish) Anonymous

Food between Friends by Jesse Tyler Ferguson and Julie Tanous

Home Cooking and *More Home Cooking* by Laurie Colwin

Chaat: Recipes from the Kitchens, Markets, and Railways of India by Maneet Chauhan

Food52: Genius Recipes: 100 Recipes That Will Change the Way You Cook by Kristen Miglore

The Pioneer Woman Cooks by Ree Drummond

Georgia Cooking in an Oklahoma Kitchen by Trisha Yearwood with Gwen Yearwood and Beth Yearwood Bernard

Modern Comfort Food by Ina Garten

The Taste of Southern Cooking by Edna Lewis

The Woks of Life by the Leung Family

How to Eat by Nigella Lawson

Mastering the Art of French Cooking by Julia Child, Louisette Bertholle, and Simone Beck

The Cloister Walk by Kathleen Norris

The Western Canon by Harold Bloom

Race Matters by Cornel West

Women Talking by Miriam Toews

The Murder at the Vicarage by Agatha Christie

The Wedding Date by Jasmine Guillory

Tales of the City by Armistead Maupin

The Royal We by Heather Cocks and Jessica Morgan

As I Lay Dying by William Faulkner

Daisy Jones and The Six by Taylor Jenkins Reid

Middlemarch by George Eliot

Ulysses by James Joyce

The Corrections by Jonathan Franzen

The Road to Middlemarch by Rebecca Mead

Infinite Jest by David Foster Wallace

Pilgrims in Their Own Land: 500 Years of Religion in America by Martin Marty

Portnoy's Complaint by Philip Roth

Better Homes and Gardens

Hustler

Entertainment Weekly

Gone Girl by Gillian Flynn

The Dress Lodger by Sheri Holman

New York Trilogy by Paul Auster

On Earth We're Briefly Gorgeous by Ocean Vuong

"The Lottery" by Shirley Jackson

The Thing around Your Neck by Chimamanda Ngozi Adichie

Banished from Johnstown by Cody McDevitt

Lincoln in the Bardo by George Saunders

The Giver by Lois Lowry

Our Town by Thornton Wilder

Spoon River Anthology by Edgar Lee Masters

State of Wonder by Ann Patchett

Sense and Sensibility by Jane Austen

The Art of Losing: Poems of Grief and Healing by Kevin Young

The Eyre Affair by Jasper Fforde

Life after Life by Kate Atkinson

Olive Kitteridge by Elizabeth Strout

"Black Men and Public Space" by Brent Staples

The Universal Classic Monster Series

"The Monkey's Paw" by W. W. Jacobs

"The Monkey" by Stephen King

Rebecca by Daphne du Maurier

"All Summer in a Day" by Ray Bradbury

"The Tell-Tale Heart" by Edgar Allan Poe

On the Beach by Nevil Shute

Dracula by Bram Stoker

Carmilla by Sheridan Le Fanu

Interview with the Vampire by Anne Rice

Being Mortal by Atul Gawande

"Thanks" by W. S. Merwin

"Casabianca" by Elizabeth Bishop

"God Says Yes to Me" by Kaylin Haught

A Year in Poetry: A Treasury of Classic and Modern Verses for Every Date on the Calendar, edited by Thomas E. Foster and Elizabeth C. Guthrie

"The Impertinence of the Thing" by John Mole

"Paul Revere's Ride" by Henry Wadsworth Longfellow

"The Battle of Bennington" by William Cullen Bryant

Twelfth Night by William Shakespeare

"An American Tradition" by Joyce Carol Oates

"15th February" by Peter Reading

"To Autumn" by John Keats

King Henry V by William Shakespeare

John Brown's Body by Stephen Vincent Benét

"Another Troy" by Alice Fulton

"Don Larsen's Perfect Game" by Paul Goodman

"What the Engines Said" by Bret Harte

"Having Arrived by Bike at Battery Park" by Grace Paley

"Kings' Day, 1984" by Richard Katrovas

Poetry 180, edited by Billy Collins

Blue Iris: Poems and Essays by Mary Oliver

Ireland's Love Poems, edited by A. Norman Jeffares

American Religious Poetry: An Anthology by Harold Bloom

Out on a Leash by Shirley MacLaine and Terry MacLaine

The Day I Shot Cupid by Jennifer Love Hewitt

The Anatomy of a Human Body by William J. Cheselden

ACKNOWLEDGMENTS

I was roundly mocked for thanking everyone under the sun in my last book, so I'll try to be more circumspect here: thank you to everyone, everywhere, except those who were of no help.

Kidding, kidding. I'm going to be loquacious as usual because I have ever so many reasons to be thankful, and just like the Costanzas on Festivus with their list of grievances, you folks are gonna hear about them.

I'll begin by thanking my wonderful agent, Bonnie Nadell, who believed in me and my writing exactly when I needed someone sharp, smart, and kind to do so. Thank you so much, Bonnie, for all of the immense hard work and faith. Thanks, too, to her associate Lauren Christiansen, who boosted this project wholeheartedly from the start. Of course, I'm also thankful to my wonderful editor John Glynn, who saw potential in me and this project, and brought us both to Hanover Square Press. John is a delight—supportive, just challenging enough, and unafraid to add the notation "Can you make this funnier?" in the margins. More thanks to Eden Railsback at Hanover Square, for ably coordinating so many moving parts and cheering the book on, and to Laura Gianino, publicist extraordinaire, as well. My thanks also to copyeditor Vanessa Wells, and proofreader Sophia Kostanski, who made my burbling aeons better.

Epically huge thanks to the gifted writers who so kindly blurbed the book: Annabelle Gurwitch, Caitlin Kunkel, Mary Norris, Elizabeth Passarella, Jen Spyra and David L. Ulin. Thanks, too, to the wonderful mensch George Saunders for his help. And thanks to all of my fellow humor-writing chicks: Caitlin Kunkel, Devorah Blachor, Brooke Preston, and many more than I can name.

Turning to my other career, I have huge gratitude for all of the good folks at the University of Pittsburgh. Thank you especially to Jeff Oaks, who has been wonderfully supportive of my writing, teaching, and grumbling for lo, over a decade now. Deep thanks, too, to Gayle Rogers, who nimbly balances being friend and mentor, and is alone amongst my bosses for never asking me to maybe tone it down a little. I'm grateful for the friendship and support of my fellow Writing Program faculty, especially Irina Reyn, who always asks about the book first. Thank you, too, to my other colleagues in the English department, especially Dana Ochs, Amy Murray Twyning, Sarah Elizabeth Baumann, Brenda Whitney, Marylou Gramm, and Jess FitzPatrick. Thank you, Renee Prymus, for long conversations at various Highland Park locations. Thanks to the departmental office staff for putting up with my whims, including sudden desires to microwave meals at 4:55 p.m.

I'm deeply grateful to my students, without whom I would have very little material, and a sad, lonely, quiet life. Teaching you restores my hope in humanity, gives me a great deal of personal pleasure, and allows me to fool myself into believing that I have not aged a day past twenty-seven. To all of you from the RLC, WMS, Stella, BTA, and Pitt, I am grateful for your help, your kindness, your good humor, and your incredible insights into literature that I get to pass off as my own next semester. Thank you. Please keep reading.

Pittsburgh has a lovely writing community, of which White Whale Bookstore and City Books are the twin pillars of light, in my estimation. Thank you to both, especially Arlan Hess at City, whose friendship and support are perfectly done. I'm grateful to Adrian Es Ramírez of the *Pittsburgh Post-Gazette* (and of the Facebook), too. And beyond the city limits, thank you to all of the librarians at all of the libraries where I've found best friends for all the years of my life. You are too numerous to name; your work is deeply important and valued. Thank you.

I'm grateful to my frequent editors Emma Allen at the *New Yorker*, and Chris Monks and Lucy Huber at *McSweeney's Internet Tendency* for making my writing stronger and better. I learn from you every single time we work together. Thanks.

I suffered a round of scary symptoms and difficult diagnoses while at work on this book, and I'm more aware than ever that good health is a fragile, precious thing. Thank you to those who have helped restore mine, at least somewhat: Dr. Melissa Dosch; Dr. Deborah Co; Dr. Joseph Cillo; Dr. Jason

Choorapuzha; Dr. Bridget Hathaway; Dr. Khahn Nguyen; Dr. Lisa Pawelski; Dr. Daniela Schwartz; Lisa Wood, PA; and Cassandra Jakubick, PT. Thank you as well to the churches and pastors I turn to for spiritual support: St. Andrew Lutheran Church, Pittsburgh; Mount Calvary Lutheran Church, Johnstown; the Washington National Cathedral; the Reverend Melissa Larsen Stoller.

Thank you to the Swick/Ellington gang in South Carolina for your unfailing support, and to Meadow Fallon-Dora, Brett Sullivan Santry, Kristin Link, Joy and David Givens, the Larsen-Stollers, and other Pittsburgh friends for lunches out, Pirates games, and similar distractions from the demands of teaching and writing. Thank you to my Facebook friends, and Tweeps, and Insta… uh, homies? I don't know, but I love being in the muck of social media with you, especially my Former Prom Date Matteo.

Thank you, as absolutely always, to the Brooklyn gang: Suzie Agins, Casey Weaver, Mark Snyder, and the California contingent of Victoria Libertore and Jen Koltin, with special thanks to Duck Migge and Gordon Cox for hosting what is inevitably the funnest night of my quarter when I'm in town.

Thank you to Danielle Duffy and Erica Giglio-Pac; I was once told that teacher friendships don't last for a year past when you work together. I'm so glad we're still proving that wrong. I'm grateful to all of my former teaching colleagues, too. It was good to work with you.

Christine Marr, thank you for your cheerleading and true-blue friendship. I still miss sitting around the Courtright Library with you, thirty years later. Love you. To Avery and Caden: Egg.

Thank you to my personal MedFriend Uber, Gretel Kalten-baugh. She is okay. Also, thank you, Ma and Pa K. Love you all.

Thank you to my aunties Nedra and Gladys, and my Aunt Linda and Uncle Pete, for always being interested in me.

Andrew Hansen continues to excel at best friendship: he is kind, funny, supportive, perpetually on my side, intelligent and just wicked enough. I can never thank him enough, and not just because he and Corey have saved me thousands of dollars on New York hotels. Everyone mentioned so far is someone I love, or would love, to talk books with, but Roo, I love to talk about absolutely *anything* with you. Thank you for our thirty-year conversation. I love you.

Thank you to Justin, the best little brother around: steady, kind, smart, funny. Thanks, Poopie. And thanks to Kate, aka Mrs. Poopie, too. And thanks to Freda, dog niece extraordinaire, who seems to always know when I need to pet her and stare off into the middle distance. Love you three.

I miss my grandparents so much, and in writing this book thought especially often of my grandmother Kathryn Downin Zeger, who taught me to read and thus made so much of my life possible. I love and miss you, Mum-mum.

My dad, the Reverend Ronald B. Reed, pops up in this book again and again, a sign, I'm sure, of how much I miss him, and how much my life was shaped by him. Love and miss you, Dad.

That leaves my mom, Gloria Reed, without whom I would be underfed, perpetually late, emotionally bereft, and very sad. She has facilitated me and my work for lo, these nearly fifty years. Thank you, Mom, for making sure I always have enough: books, meals, money, friendship, love. I love you.